The
Well-Read
Mom

Read More. Read Well.

By Marcie Stokman, M.A.,
Founder of Well-Read Mom

ISBN 978-1-7339423-2-4

Published by Well-Read Mom Press

Illustrations by Andy Grams/Design Solutions
Author photo by Josie Vouk

Layout, Design & Production by Chip & Jean Borkenhagen
River Place Press
Aitkin, MN

Printed by Bang Printing
Brainerd, MN

This project was made possible by a grant provided by the Five
Wings Arts Council with funds from the McKnight Foundation.

Praise for
The Well-Read Mom

Marcie Stokman personally embodies the principle that gave rise to her international reading movement: "The good we do for the people around us springs from the life inside us." Saint John Paul II thought that women had a principle role in restoring true leisure to our frenetic, distracted, and soulless culture. Marcie is doing just that as she encourages her band of well-read women to nourish their minds and souls, and "reconnect to God, and the big picture of creation, life, and love - the things that really matter." Now, anyone who has already profited from Marcie's efforts, or wishing to do so for the first time, can read her and learn the reasons for restoring the lost art of leisure.

—Margaret Harper McCarthy, Editor of *Humanum:*
Issues in Family, Culture, and Science and Associate
Professor of Theology at the Pontifical John Paul II Institute

Well-Read Mom isn't just for moms. Nor is it just for the well-read. This is a delightful, insightful, and inspiring book on how, why, and what to read. It is suitable for anyone who desires more motivation and more skills in gleaning the goodness that good literature offers. Full of age-old wisdom and practical tips, this is a book I will recommend widely.

—Karen Swallow Prior, award-winning English Professor and author
of *On Reading Well: Finding the Good Life through Great Books*
and *Fierce Convictions: The Extraordinary Life of Hannah
More—Poet, Reformer, Abolitionist*

In an age of tweets and texts, Marcie Stokman presents a powerful case for the value of literature. Hers is an empowering, uplifting invitation to return to great books, which like great art, cultivate the mind and awaken the soul.

—Elizabeth Lev, bestselling author of *How Catholic Art Saved the Faith*

Marcie's book is full of contrasts: accessible, yet profound; deeply personal, yet universal (there's probably not a mom in the world that can't resonate with the story of taking Beth to her ballet lesson!). By drawing on her experience to illustrate the profound importance of beauty, reflection, and a true experience of leisure, this book ignites the desire to live more deeply and intentionally.

—Kimberly C. Shankman, Dean of Benedictine College,
Atchison, Kansas

I raised my four children in the '80s and '90s, an era when children began being packed off to day-care while their moms flooded the workforce. Suddenly, the neighborhoods were ghost-towns during the week with no kids for my children to play with, no other stay-at-home moms for me to talk to. I remember feeling isolated, lonely and depressed, as if I had been cast up on a desert island. I remember going for days without talking to another adult other than my husband or the cashier in the grocery store. How I longed for interesting conversation that did not include the words "potty" or "no". What a life-line 'Well-Read Mom' would have been to me then. Now stay-at-home moms can be part of a nationwide community of readers who come together in local groups to discuss good books. In a culture increasingly polarized by special interest groups and opposing ideologies, Marcie Stokman, founder of Well-Read Mom, has single-handedly brought back the civilized—and civilizing—tradition of authentic conversation. It is a gift of inestimable value.

—Suzanne M. Wolfe, award-winning author of *Murder by Any Name*

When we tilt toward a new "dark age" in terms of literature and even mere literacy, storytelling increasingly becomes both the province of a talented-if-insular few and the product of a market preying upon human proclivities toward sentimentality. Through her stunningly successful labor of love *The Well-Read Mom*, Marcie Stokman has restored to literature its rightful readership of everyman—or, in this case, every mom. Through an admixture of biographical backdrop, philosophical underpinnings, and practical tips, Stockman makes it clear that deprived of a community through which we can grasp the good things that great books give us, our parenting is impoverished. When we take short "retreats" from the fray of child-rearing, when we converse upon literature that is either broadly enduring or charged with a Catholic vision, our hearts expand and our souls widen. Deepened by our ability to see the part in relation to the whole, to see the unseen through the seen, we can be better characters in the drama of our own little lives.

—Joshua Hren, Ph.D., founder of Wiseblood Books and
author of *This Our Exile: Short Stories*

Marcie Stokman's book is a welcome apologia for a return to the disciplined reading of the great works of literature. In these beautifully written pages, women will find relief, permission, and encouragement to pursue a life of deep reading for themselves, their families, and the culture.

—Elizabeth M. Kelly, award-winning author of *Jesus Approaches:
What Contemporary Women Can Learn about Healing,
Freedom and Joy from the Women of the New Testament*

In this important little book, Marcie and her friends invite us to a life that is richer in imagination, companionship and empathy and, thus, so much richer in meaning. And who are her friends? Moms from Minnesota, and moms from Tennessee, and moms from Texas...and Dads...and college professors...and students...and Willa Cather, and Dorothy Day, and Victor Hugo, and Dante, and Tolkien, and Lewis, and Tolstoy...and all of the timeless characters and truths they have bequeathed to those who take the time to pay attention. Marcie witnesses that such time and attention are possible, and invaluable, for all of us.

—Reverend Richard Veras, Director of Pastoral Formation, Archdiocese of New York, author of *Word Made Flesh* and regular contributor to *Magnificat* magazine

Marcie Stokman has made reading books once again a popular past time, at least among a small and growing set of essential believers—*moms*. Her apology for the necessity of reading great books echoes the encouragement of centuries, and she does well to repeat it to us now. As the founder of book clubs that now span the country, a mom herself, and a devotee of beautiful literature, Stokman creates reading lists with substance, depth, and challenge. In her book, she connects such reading with virtuous living. Who knew that reading a novel could be a path to being a good mom? For Stokman, reading nourishes the soul, giving us more with which to feed those young souls around us. With practical advice and vulnerable examples of her own failures and successes, Stokman inspires us to love well, to think well, to be what we all desire but assume we have too little time to become— well-read moms.

—Jessica Hooten Wilson, recipient of the 2019 Hiett Prize in the Humanities and award-winning author of *Giving the Devil his Due: Demonic Authority in the Fiction of Flannery O'Connor and Fyodor Dostoevsky*

Dedication

To Pete

*"And roots, if they are to bear fruits,
must be kept well in the soil of the land."*
—Pearl S. Buck, *The Good Earth*

*"There is nothing more admirable than when two people who
see eye to eye keep house as man and wife, confounding their
enemies and delighting their friends."*
—Homer, *The Odyssey*

*"It's by understanding me, and the boys, and mother,
that you have helped me. I expect that is the only way
one person ever really can help another."*
—Willa Cather, *O Pioneers!*

*"O magnify the Lord with me, and let us
exalt his name together."*
—Ps. 34:3

Thank you for being my companion, my roots, my ally. Thank you
for your quiet strength and practical wisdom. It is my joy and honor
to be on this journey together.

Table of Contents

Acknowledgments

Thank you McKnight Foundation and the Five Wings Arts Council for helping this book become a reality. Receiving this grant gave me what I needed to start writing: 10 days of quiet at St. John's University. Thank you Mary Teck; your grant-writing expertise started this adventure.

As I sat in front of my laptop with stacks of my articles, piles of papers and messy notes, I was ready to begin but my mind went blank. I wondered how I could have writer's block before I had even begun. It already felt too hard. Thank you Morgan Smith for joining me at St. John's to sort through the papers and come up with an outline. Thank you to my friend and publicist Krista Soukup for encouraging me when I lacked confidence and giving me the springboard to begin writing. Thank you, Chip and Jean Borkenhagen, for designing and publishing this work. The two of you go the extra mile with diligence, grace, and excellence. You are true artists, and I thank you for the beauty you have brought to this book. Thank you Andy Grams for lending beauty to the pages with your artwork.

Thank you to Tracey Finck, who 25 years prior had asked, "Are you a writer?" Because I liked Tracey immediately, I answered with confidence, "I could be, what do you have in mind?" From that time on, Tracey and I have worked on many projects together culminating with this book. Thank you for bringing order and a narrative arc to my ramblings, for persevering to the end and for your patient but firm ability to keep me on track. Thanks to Sam Nelson, Susan Severson, Sarah Steinke and Alison Solove for your draft reading support.

Thank you to Cecelia Burgwald for your idea sketches. From the start you've been sketching with Well-Read Mom and we've always loved the spunk they bring. Thanks to Sarah Steinke who wrote the copy and book promotion materials with creative fervor.

Thanks to all the women in Well-Read Mom and my own group who keep me reading and laughing.

To the fantastic WRM team: Colleen Hutt, Janel Lewandowski, Nicole Bugnaki, Susan Severson, Alison Solove, and Nadine Schaefbaurer. You give so much above and beyond. You are dedicated to the mission. I am grateful to live a beautiful friendship together in this work. Thank you to my daughter Beth whose desires for friendship and reading deeply ignited the Well-Read Mom journey. Thanks to Stephanie, whose understanding of our need for beauty birthed our logo and design. Thank you to Lisa, Margaret and Emma who have helped with all kinds of details.

Finally, thanks to my family for sacrificing in so many ways so I could write. Thank you for the privilege of being your mom. Thank you to my dear husband, Peter; it is a privilege to share this journey with you.

Foreword

Eight years ago Well-Read Mom did not exist. It would never have existed if my mom hadn't followed her desire to read good literature herself and to help other women do so also. For those of us who are in Well-Read Mom, it's crazy to think of the last eight years of life without Well-Read Mom. How would I ever have gotten through another Minnesota winter without my dear and crazy friend Beret from *Giants of the Earth*?! Or embraced the experience of putting on my toddler's shoes for the thousandth time without the story of St. Therese in my heart? Or folded laundry without reciting Dante's *Purgatorio*? Just kidding about that last one. But reading Dante was one of the most beautiful struggles I've gone through, and that never would have happened without Well-Read Mom. Dante's images and ideas of the afterlife still illuminate my mind . . . sometimes even while I'm folding laundry!

When something is exploding in numbers, followings, likes, hearts, whatever it is, it's worth asking, "What is happening here?" Sometimes the answer is rather base and discouraging, but other times it's something I wouldn't want to miss. Consider reading this book with that question in mind: "What's happening here?"

Well-Read Mom went from 0 to 900 women in the first couple years. It was an—almost unintended—explosion of numbers. We were creating Well-Read Mom for ourselves, out of our own desire to read more and to be with our friends, and women were jumping on board at an exponential rate. So one must ask, "What is happening here?" Why do women want to read? How has this book club become such a meaningful part of women's lives? And how is it that so many women, all busy as moms, professionals, daughters, sisters, et cetera, have found the time and energy to read good literature and to discuss it with friends?

I am forever grateful that my mom followed her desire and struck out to start something new. By helping me to read good books together with friends, Well-Read Mom has introduced me to stories, characters, and ideas—and friendships—that have truly changed my life. Whether you've been with us from the beginning or are just hearing about Well-Read Mom for the first time, I trust that it can do the same for you.

Bethany Nelson, co-founder of Well-Read Mom

Introduction

In the fall of 2012, when 22 women gathered in my living room for the start of Well-Read Mom, we could not have imagined that eight years later these little groups would be duplicated in almost every state across the country and in Canada.

In such a culture as ours, would women really be interested in the proposal to read books from the Western tradition together? Resoundingly, the answer has been yes! What started from a need to accompany each other in reading books, what started from a desire and longing for my daughter and daughter-in-law to meet with other women in a meaningful, intelligent way, what started from a desire to grow in friendship, have fun, and yet be intellectually challenged—all this has grown into something of a movement, the modest beginnings of a cultural force. The book you hold in your hands is born of gratitude for that *yes*.

Engaging women to read more and read well is one key to cultural change. Being accompanied makes it easier to move towards what is good, beautiful, and true. Would any of us have read Homer's *Odyssey*, Dante's *Divine Comedy* or Hugo's *Les Misérable* on our own? Friendship and accountability are making the difference.

Today, books from our tradition are being pushed aside for more contemporary works, which do offer value but cannot replace the treasure of the traditional canon. Moreover, people tend to ignore literature altogether because they think it's irrelevant. In particular, reading from print is falling by the wayside. It's becoming harder to garner the necessary focus and attention for sustained reading.

But we in Well-Read Mom are a group of women who want more than we're offered by the status quo. We disagree with the perceived assumptions that classic novels are no longer relevant and that reading books from print is out of date. Good books are always in season. And not only is this literature valid, it is also nourishment for human development. Our own hearts, emotions, and imaginations need to be educated.

We are raising the bar because we are raising children.

We are helping to form their minds and hearts by being intentional in forming our own. We have discovered a treasure not only for ourselves but also for our families and communities.

Wherever you are in your reading journey, join us. If you don't consider yourself a reader, I hope you'll reconsider. By staying together in a disciplined way, women, even those who can only read a few chapters a month, are reaping the rewards.

It was Dorothy Day who said, "I'm not great at analyzing those novels; I want to live by them."

She did!

Dorothy Day lived an exceptional life.

It is my hope that by taking our lives seriously and by reading together, you and I will live exceptional lives, too.

PART ONE
THE STORY

"You don't need to see the whole staircase. Just take the first step."

—Dr. Martin Luther King Jr.

Chapter 1

The Birth of Well-Read Mom

STUMBLING UPON A NEED

In the spring of 2012, three different mothers' groups asked me to come and give a talk. Since I had already spoken to some of these women about children's literature, I thought it would be interesting to speak about personal reading and get a feel for what books women were reading for themselves. I titled the talk "Well-Read Mom."

Turns out I hit a nerve.

For most of the mothers I talked to, personal reading was a luxury they had sacrificed in the name of family. In fact, not one woman in any of those groups was reading quality literature for her own enjoyment and growth.

Many of them weren't happy about it. Some felt embarrassed, others felt guilty. Most just accepted it as normal.

When I asked the women why they weren't reading, hands crept up hesitantly. One by one, they explained, lamented, and justified why reading was impossible, given the demands of daily life. "I don't have time," of course, was the main reason these women weren't reading. But I also heard comments like these:

- "I sometimes read a self-help book or a spiritual bestseller because I can justify that. But at this time in my life, reading literature feels selfish."
- "I was never a good reader in high school."
- "I'd like to read, but I wouldn't have a clue where to start."
- "My family watches TV at night because that is something we can do together. If I get a book out, I feel like I'm isolating myself from my kids, so we watch TV instead. At least we can do that together."
- "In my family, we're all on our own devices, even during dinner.

We fill our plates in the kitchen and then go to our own rooms to eat in front of our TVs and phones." This comment was shared by a woman with tears in her eyes.

Of the women attending the talks, only one said she regularly read fiction, but she felt bad because she knew the quality of books she was reading was sub-par: "I know there are better books out there, but I have no idea where to start, so I pick up whatever bestseller looks good at the grocery store."

Each time, as I drove home from one of these events, the faces of the women who had shared came to mind. Jean, Sarah, Sally, Jen—all these women cared deeply about mothering. They wanted to nurture their children. They were trying their best to stay afloat in family life. They had come to the talk looking for support and encouragement. Then I waltzed in, spouting off statistics about the importance of personal reading. I'm sure to them I may as well have been saying, "Hi, I'm here to show you one more way you are not measuring up as a mom!"

How is this little talk I just gave going to make a bit of difference in anyone's life? I pondered. *It won't! The only thing it will do is make the women feel like there's one more thing they might be failing at.*

Women, including me, wanted to read more, but none of us knew how to take a step toward that goal. I started thinking about my own life, and I realized that I was actually in the same boat. While I could talk about the importance of good books, in all honesty I wasn't reading literature on a regular basis either. We were all missing out on something beautiful. I drove home sad.

SEARCHING FOR A SOLUTION

I thought back to my own experience. I had a foundation in reading because I had had the good fortune to be in a reading group in years past. For over 10 years, I faithfully attended a book club with a small group of friends. We read the classics and other good books. When we first started the book club, I was barely treading water as a mom. With four little ones clamoring for attention, I needed an activity to call my own. I needed to get out of the house and have some intelligent adult conversation. I needed a reading challenge and accountability. Book club provided a way to meet with friends on a consistent basis. I looked forward to it. Although I knew almost nothing about the classic literature we were reading, I persevered. These were the books my friends wanted to read, and I wanted to be with these people.

I was scared at first because I didn't know how to "analyze" literature. But once I started reading, I found that I didn't need to analyze the books. I could just listen as the books spoke to me. I let myself get caught up in the story and the lives of the characters. I found that this type of receptive reading was having a good effect on my heart. I felt inspired to live like Jean Valjean from *Les Misérables*, Father Zosima from *The Brothers Karamazov*, and Kitty from *Anna Karenina*. Reading about their lives awoke in me a desire for greatness of soul!

The conversations at book club were also helping me. Because of our in-depth discussions, I came to understand myself in new ways. I enjoyed the surprising twists and turns that took place as we talked about the books and the new ideas the books had birthed in us.

My experience in this book club taught me three things.

First, I discovered I could read more than I thought I could.

Second, even if I didn't understand everything that was going on in the book (I didn't), and even if I wasn't able to finish the book (often the case), I learned that reading great books was a positive experience for me, an experience different from reading self-help books or bestseller fiction.

Third, reading with a group was different from—and better than—reading on my own.

After 10 years in this book club, we moved to another town, and I was not able to continue participating. Almost without realizing it, I left reading great literature behind. I was engaged in reading, but I wasn't having moments of connecting with literature in a profound way.

In addition to feeling sad about stirring up guilt in the women who attended my talks, I also felt like a hypocrite. I was giving presentations that I called "Well-Read Mom" when that title did not describe me at the time.

And then it hit me—I had used the phrase "Well-Read Mom" because that's what I wanted to be. I wanted to be well-read. And I was looking for help.

Driving home from speaking to these groups of young moms, I understood I needed to change. Reading literature was life-giving; I was missing out. And now it was clear to me that many other women were missing out, too.

I Wasn't Alone

Several days later, my daughter Beth, a new mom at the time, called me almost in tears. "Mom, I've had it with these mother's groups. I've been to this group three times, and all they talk about is what kind of diapers to buy. It's all about the kids. Mom, isn't there a place after college where women get together and actually talk about the real questions of life?" I heard a cry in Beth's voice.

Her longing for more merged with my own, and the idea for Well-Read Mom was born.

The concept was simple. I offered to put together a list of books for us to read together over the next few years. She agreed to gather some friends in St. Paul, where she was living, and I would invite some of my friends in Crosby to join with me. Our two little book groups would stay together. We'd help each other be accountable.

This new avenue for friendship ignited a passion in me. Putting a plan together became a work of joy. I went to my bookshelves and pulled all the books I thought might be interesting to women. Spreading them out on the floor, I counted over 150 books. Hmm. Where to start?

I was pumped about this idea; I hoped it would be a long-term reading adventure. Maybe we could read all the great classics of the Western tradition—books by Homer, Virgil, St. Augustine, and

Dante—in chronological order. But that idea was so overwhelming that now I had a problem: I didn't want to be in this club! The thought of tackling those difficult works one after the other made me feel like giving up before I started. Could I really ask my friends to join a book club whose first selection was *The Iliad*? This idea would be over before it started. It would be like asking the women to run a marathon when we needed to start jogging to the stop sign and back.

The Rule of St. Benedict came to mind. In the sixth century, when St. Benedict wrote his famous Rule, he intended that an abbot should govern his monastery in such a way so that "the strong have something to yearn for and the weak have nothing to run from."

That's what I wanted for myself and my daughter and our friends—a hospitable place where one woman might experience the great classics for the first time, and another, perhaps already a voracious reader, could continue to grow. The idea would be to raise the bar without crushing anyone. A tall order, but possible.

The following passage from St. Pope John Paul II's "Letter to Women" inspired the yearly themes for Well-Read Mom:

"This word of thanks to the Lord for his mysterious plan regarding the vocation and mission of women in the world is at the same time a concrete and direct word of thanks to women, to every woman, for all that they represent in the life of humanity.

"Thank you, women who are mothers! You have sheltered human beings within yourselves in a unique experience of joy and travail. This experience makes you become God's own smile upon the newborn child, the one who guides your child's first steps, who helps it to grow, and who is the anchor as the child makes its way along the journey of life.

"Thank you, women who are wives! You irrevocably join your future to that of your husbands, in a relationship of mutual giving, at the service of love and life.

"Thank you, women who are daughters and women who are sisters! Into the heart of the family, and then of all society, you bring the richness of your sensitivity, your intuitiveness, your generosity and fidelity.

"Thank you, women who work! You are present and active in every area of life-social, economic, cultural, artistic and political. In this way you make an indispensable contribution to the growth of a culture which unites reason and feeling, to a model of life ever open to the sense of "mystery," to the establishment of economic and political structures ever more worthy of humanity.

"Thank you, consecrated women! Following the example of the greatest of women, the Mother of Jesus Christ, the Incarnate Word, you open yourselves with obedience and fidelity to the gift of God's love. You help the Church and all mankind to experience a "spousal" relationship to God, one which magnificently expresses the fellowship which God wishes to establish with his creatures.

"Thank you, every woman, for the simple fact of being a woman! Through the insight which is so much a part of your womanhood, you enrich the world's understanding and help to make human relations more honest and authentic."

—From the Vatican, June 29, 1995,
the Solemnity of Saints Peter and Paul.
JOHN PAUL II

CHOOSING THE SELECTIONS

Still, the problem was how to order the selections.

One day, the answer came. I was reading Pope John Paul's 1995 "Letter to Women." He was thanking women in their various capacities, enumerating their many roles in life: mothers, daughters, workers, sisters, wives, etc. As I read, I nearly jumped out of my chair; this could be the way to categorize the books! We could organize them loosely around these capacities inherent in being a woman. The first year could be Year of the Daughter, and then we could follow with Year of the Mother, then, Year of the Spouse, Year of the Worker, Year of the Friend, etc. This provided a framework for choosing the books.

That first year, I chose classic fiction whose characters included daughters. During Advent and Lent, I wanted to read spiritual classics, and during the month of November—when I knew we would all be busy with holiday preparations—some short stories.

My daughter-in-law Steph got excited about the idea, too. I remember a wonderful moment when Steph, Beth, and I were sitting around my kitchen table drinking coffee and chatting about our plans to start these parallel book clubs. Steph offered to design an invitation: "If we are going to do this for women, it needs to be beautiful!" I was surprised how her desire to make beautiful invitations moved me. Attention to beauty was a way to honor the women. Steph drew, freehand, a cameo of a woman reading a book. We added a tag-line that sort of summed up what we were trying to accomplish together: "Read More, Read Well."

And just like that, we had a brand, without even realizing it. Steph also included the little mission statement we came up with as we sat around my kitchen table: "A book club to encourage, equip, and educate women through literature from the Western and Catholic Tradition."

Looking back, I see what an important step this was to make the invitations beautiful. Mother Teresa said, "Make whatever you do something beautiful for God." Even if only a few women responded, we wanted them to know that we were setting out on a noble venture, worthy of our best efforts. We wanted to invite them to participate in something beautiful.

We printed about 40 invitations. I addressed 22 to friends I thought might enjoy this book club. Beth and Steph sent some to their friends in the Twin Cities. And another friend, Laura, heard me talking about the idea and invited her friends in St. Cloud, Minnesota, to start a third group.

INVITING THE WOMEN

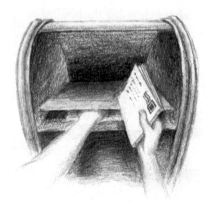

But then I suddenly got cold feet. I remember standing at the blue mailbox on Main Street with my arm half-way in the box, unable to drop the invites. A wave of fear came over me; I clutched the postcards tight, afraid to take this risk.

If I let go of these, it means we are really going to start this. *Who do I think I am to invite women to a club where I introduce the books? I'm not an expert. I only took one literature class in college. I'm an amateur.*

I summoned my courage and countered the fear. *But women aren't reading, and neither am I. We'll be happier if we read more. These books were written for ordinary people like me. What can it hurt to try?*

I really wanted to read good books, and I wanted to do it with other women. My desire rose. The postcards dropped.

PREPARING FOR THE FIRST GATHERING

If we were really going to start this thing, I needed to prepare.

I had promised Beth that if she led a group in St. Paul, I would record an audio introduction for each book and email it to her so she could play it at her meeting. I also offered to write and send discussion questions. This would save her the work of preparing for the meetings.

Our first selection was "The Birthmark," a short story by Nathaniel Hawthorne. I did a bit of research, just to give us some context, to have a little guidance regarding the themes we might look for. I knew we weren't trying to become literary critics. But I wanted to share enough information to spark an interest and get started on the work.

Ultimately, I hoped reading the selections would open the door to conversation and connection. I hoped that the friendships, as well as the books, would help us grow in wisdom.

September 12, 2012, was the night of my group's introductory meeting in Crosby. I had invited 22 women. How many would actually come? I prepared coffee, trusting that I wouldn't be spending the evening alone. At 7:30, I found myself in my living room surrounded by 22 women. Everyone came! That was the first official meeting of Well-Read Mom. I welcomed the women joining in this adventure, and I knew their hearts were like mine.

FINDING A MENTOR

One day, while researching online as I prepared an introduction for the next book, I came across a two-volume set entitled *The Encyclopedia of Catholic Literature* by Dr. Mary Reichardt. Her name sounded familiar. Two of my kids had taken a class from a Dr. Reichardt at the University of St. Thomas. Could this be the same Reichardt?

Sure enough.

I called her up. Dr. Reichardt graciously agreed to meet with me to talk through book selections. Many times since that initial meeting,

Dr. Reichardt and I have met to go over books. Her breadth and depth of knowledge about literature have been a gift to us at Well-Read Mom. With Dr. Reichardt's help, we fine-tuned the initial lists for the various years.

THE FIRST CONFERENCE

Dr. Reichardt offered to give a talk for us on Kristin Lavransdatter, one of the winter selections the first year. That sounded wonderful. The women from the three groups could come together. It would be like a conference.

The only problem was that I couldn't think of a place for our three groups to gather that wasn't a church basement. It needed to be a special and beautiful place.

I thought, *Why not call the University of St. Thomas? Several of my kids were students there. I could at least try.*

Another scary moment.

I remember pacing with my phone before calling the university to ask about hosting a conference. This may not sound like a difficult thing to do, but I had been a stay-at-home mom for years, and calling up a university felt daunting. *What will I say? And anyway, who am I to initiate a conference on literature at a university?* After pacing back and forth, fighting the fear, I told myself that it was reasonable to ask. *The purpose is for women to grow. Why would a university not want to encourage women to read?* Again, my desire rose, and with it, courage. I made the call. Before I knew it, we were scheduled to host the first Well-Read Mom Conference.

On a bitterly cold afternoon in January 2013, eighty-one women from around Minnesota gathered at the University of St. Thomas. In addition to members of the three initial groups, we were joined by other interested women. I looked around at these women and was again struck by the realization that their hearts were the same as mine.

THE IDEA GROWS

After the conference, 21 new groups started. What we were proposing was resonating with women.

The following year, 2013-14, over 200 women in over 60 groups joined us. Well-Read Mom has continued to grow—mostly through word of mouth—ever since. As I write this book, we are in our eighth year with more than 400 groups gathering throughout the country.

Month by month, we set out with the goal to read and then compare the reading with our personal experience. Through this process, we come to understand more about our own lives. Rather than becoming literary critics, we are reading books for our own growth, to widen our often-narrow perspective and understanding of others, and to awaken our desire for greatness of soul.

GROWING PAINS

I am inspired every single time I meet with my group, every year at our conference, every time I visit another Well-Read Mom group and meet the women who share a passion to read and grow.

But let me tell you what does not inspire me.

Paperwork.

The paperwork started when, in our second year, we decided to publish a Reading Companion booklet. Of course, it costs money to print and distribute, so we needed to start charging for membership. And the website became more complicated, so I needed to hire help. Three years into Well-Read Mom, it became clear that we needed to form as a 501(c)(3) nonprofit organization. This was a complicated operation. My sister-in-law Janel offered to help me fill out the stacks of different forms involved.

What a project! We had papers strewn all over her table and on every space we could find. I sat there perplexed and paralyzed, not knowing how to move ahead.

"You seem kind of down," Janel commented.

I was down. For me, trying to understand these forms was like trying to read Chinese.

"Janel," I said, "What are we doing? What if we fill out some of these legal forms wrong? This is so complicated. Someone asked me the other day what our goal is with Well-Read Mom. Honestly, at this point, my goal is to stay out of trouble. I really don't want to record these audios from jail."

We laughed. But seriously, the load with Well-Read Mom was beginning to feel heavy. I was single-handedly trying to answer every email and manage the finances. Janel and my daughter-in-law Steph were doing all they could to put a website together. This was not what I had signed up for. I wanted to encourage women to read, not run a business.

We really needed help.

CHRIST IN THE BOAT

Another day I was back in Janel's kitchen. "Janel, I feel like this boat is sinking. We don't know how to do all of this on the computer. This is beyond us."

Literally five minutes later, our friend Nadine stopped by to pick up her son Max from Janel's house. She popped her head in the door to say hi and saw we were working on Well-Read Mom. "Say, if you ever need someone to help with the computer end of things, I could do that. That's what I do."

"Excuse me? What did you say? Are you serious?" This was not a coincidence. For me, it was a monumental answer to prayer. I saw again that God was guiding this whole process.

That night, I wrote in my journal, "Lord, you sent Nadine at the exact time we were sinking. Lord, I believe You are in this boat, and with You in this boat, it cannot sink! I don't need to be afraid. I am not carrying the load by myself. You are providing."

PRAYING FOR THE WOMEN

Another time when I was experiencing the heaviness, I was sitting behind my computer answering emails, updating member addresses, and sending out packets to replace ones that had gotten lost in the mail. Every task seemed like a burden. I was making mistakes with all the details and addresses. Some women were upset with me for my errors.

I mentioned to a friend that it was getting to be too much. I expected him to tell me to get more help, to delegate more. Instead, he surprised me by asking, "Do you ever pray for these women?"

"Pray for them?" I was perplexed. "No, I don't."

"You need to," he stated with simple confidence. "Start praying for these women every day. And whenever you can, go to visit them—not because the women need to see you, but because you need to see their faces."

So I took his advice. I started to pray for the women of Well-Read Mom. As I did so, opportunities came to visit some of the groups. I saw that it was true—it was for me. It has been a great blessing to meet these women whose hearts are the same as mine, to be reminded that the work of Well-Read Mom is part of a beautiful journey.

"We read to know we're not alone."

—William Nicholson, *Shadowlands*

"Advances in technology ... have the propensity to dehumanize, ... to lead to the elimination of human interaction. In this we lose the life-giving art of friendship; we forget how to companion, how to be present, ... the literal "being there" that Christ highlights in the Incarnation."

—author Elizabeth M. Kelly

"A friend is someone with whom one shares the thirst for meaning, someone who helps you walk, someone who reminds you of what your heart is made for."

—WRM member Marcia Otto

Chapter 2

Fun, Friendship, and a Unique Format

Since starting Well-Read Mom (WRM) in my living room, I have realized that something about this model has struck a chord with women.

What is it?

Book clubs have always been around. What makes this one different?

I think it has something to do with following a unique format, prioritizing fun, and focusing on friendship.

A Unique Format

I saw right away that if our three fledgling book groups in three different towns were going to stay together, the process would need to be well-structured and easy. My daughter, a new mom when we started this venture, would only have to read the books and get her house ready. I would do the preparation.

The format we set up was that I would make a short audio recording and email it out to the other two groups to play at the beginning of the meeting. The audio would serve as a nice transition from the welcoming small talk to a focused discussion on the book.

I also sent questions they could use to jumpstart discussion if needed. The questions were designed to focus attention on how the characters and themes in the book shed light on our own life experience.

The last 10 minutes, the leader would play another recording that introduced the next month's book, giving a little background information to make it accessible and spark their interest.

The idea was to start and stop on time, keeping the official meeting to an hour and 15 minutes. Women could stay longer to chat or feel free to leave after that.

Keeping to this format has created the structure and boundaries we need to hold us accountable to our goals of really discussing these books and discovering what it is to live seriously and with greatness; it helps make this a life-giving time together, not merely the safe, surface chit-chat we can so easily slip into as busy moms.

The format also allows us to keep pace with other women across the country while at the same time growing deeper in friendship in our local communities. As women have shared their experiences with me, I've come to appreciate just how well our format supports deeper reading and fosters deeper friendships.

All this is different from other book clubs I'm aware of. The meeting format and the companion materials we offer scaffold the experience so that reading these classic works truly is happening in an hospitable way. Women have the supports, through audios, author biographies, written reflections, and highlighted themes to truly engage as much or little as they are able. We really are encouraged, equipped, and educated through our time reading and discussing together.

PRIORITIZING FUN

It might sound silly that having fun is crucial for women who want to succeed in reading quality literature. But actually, it is! Unless reading is pleasurable, we tend to avoid it. One woman told me when she finished graduate school she didn't care if she ever read another book the rest of her life. This is not unusual. I heard somewhere that over half of today's college graduates will never read another book. Why? Could it be because they have not learned to associate reading with pleasure? Maybe reading is associated with required class work, assigned book reports, and long papers; in other words, pain. In our nation, there are many school-time readers, and there are many online readers. But this is entirely different from being a nation of lifetime *book* readers.

How can we transition to an experience of pleasure while we're reading books? Having a little fun is a good place to start. For many moms, surrounded by small children 24/7, the very thought of going to someone's house, sitting on a cushioned chair, sipping hot tea, eating a warm cookie, and engaging in meaningful conversation with other interesting women sounds pretty fun. Especially when those discussions are sparked by wonderful stories that you've shared together because you've all just read the same great book!

Of course, having a memorable evening with friends discussing books won't turn us into lifetime readers overnight, but it does connect reading with pleasure, and if we reinforce this connection month after month, reading literature can become a habit for life.

FOCUSING ON FRIENDSHIP

The friendship factor is a major component in Well-Read Mom groups.

Although social media brings us constant "connection," paradoxically, it can also lead to intense isolation if being online usurps time spent actually meeting with people in the same room. While it is possible to discuss books online, we all know it is a completely different experience to sit down with women, chair-to-chair, face-to-face. The monthly gatherings and targeted discussion provide an atmosphere where friendship can take root. And the good news is, no one has to buy Tupperware for this to happen!

FACE-TO-FACE IS BETTER THAN FACEBOOK

"I first heard about Well-Read Mom over six years ago, when I was deep in the throes of the special sleep deprivation that belongs to the parents of infant twins. Even in my chronically tired state, I could feel the slow, steady atrophy of my brain brought on by a reading diet composed almost exclusively of the same toddler board books over and over again.

"When Marcie shared the book list for the second year of Well-Read Mom, I pored over that list and dreamed. I wanted to read those books. I wanted to discuss them with other women. I needed a book club, but I'd never have the energy to start one, . . . and I also didn't know a single person who would want to join me in such a cerebral activity. I had a blog at the time and a decent online community of other bookish moms, so I reached out to Marcie to see if I could start an online chapter of Well-Read Mom. I thought we'd read the books and then discuss them in a Facebook group or in the comments of my blog. I was sure she'd say yes— her mission was to encourage more moms to read well, and this seemed to me like a great way to do it.

"To my disappointment, Marcie discouraged me from doing it online. Her vision, she explained, was for face-to-face discussions where women could connect in person.

"I almost gave up, but I decided to post on Facebook just to see if anyone within driving distance might be interested in joining me. To my astonishment, someone was willing to drive to my house, and she knew someone else who might also like to come. A friend from community choir expressed interest. One more mutual friend from library story time rounded out the group. It was a small start, but as we did the work of reading the books and discussing them together, our commitment to each other and to the process of becoming better readers together strengthened our relationships. We became a community—brought together by our love of reading, but held together by our deepening friendships."

—Abbey Dupuy

I love being able to hear my neighbor's take on the main character from *My Antonia* or another friend's experience of growing up in North Dakota. I want to laugh, learn, and grow in the sense of wonder with these women whose hearts are like mine—even if their personalities and life experiences are quite different.

Helping Each Other Take the Reading Road

The road less traveled is the road that is more difficult to take—especially by myself. It is easier just to follow the crowd and do what everyone else is doing instead of thinking about living in a purposeful, intentional way. One of the benefits of a reading group is that we can take the road less traveled *together*—accompanying one another on a more difficult route but also one that will make a difference.

Only I can establish my own disciplined habit of quality reading. It is a road less traveled. Yet if I am accompanied by friends and just take one book at a time, it is easier. When I know I'm going to see my friends to discuss a book, I find myself looking forward to the discussion. I'm aware of a responsibility to at least start, and getting started is the hardest part. What I sometimes won't do for myself, I will do when it has something to do with friendship.

The friendship factor is a catalyst because when women accompany women a force is unleashed. My original goal, to actually read the books on my bookshelves, was something I couldn't do by myself. Meeting with friends is the push I need to read books like the Nobel Prize-winning, 1110-page novel *Kristin Lavransdatter*. If I didn't have a group planning to chat about this book at 7 p.m. on Saturday, I wouldn't make time to read 30 pages on Friday. Deadlines and the expectation of friends work wonders to help me read more and read well.

For me, it's like cooking. I heard about the Instant Pot from my friend Fedi. Apparently, this kitchen gadget was everything I needed to pressurize an easy, nutritious meal in minutes. Since cooking has never come easily for me, I thought this pressure-cooker would be the miracle answer. When I unwrapped my Mother's Day gift, this marvelous time-saving pot was now mine. That was nine months ago, and while all the claims of the Instant Pot are most surely true, I have yet to get the kettle out of the box. Why? New habits are difficult to form. The perceived effort required to read the instructions and figure out one more appliance seems daunting right now. So there it sits in my laundry room. What would it take for me to begin using and benefitting from that pot? It would take more than good intentions. If a group of friends came over for an Instant Pot party once a month, that would no doubt help. The threshold that needs to be pushed through is easier with the encouragement of friends.

Last May, when we began reading one of the greatest and longest novels ever published, Victor Hugo's *Les Misérables*, I found myself tempted to suggest that we all watch the movie together instead. I had enjoyed the book 20 years earlier, but this time it seemed insurmountable. But then I walked into book club and overheard my friend Linda: "I already started *Les Misérables* and it is so, so beautiful. The prose is exceptional. Every sentence! I can hardly put it down."

So much for the movie. Linda's enthusiasm for Hugo's stunning prose stirred up my desire to reread this great book. Again I was surprised how it was friendship that gave me the boost I needed. I'm so glad I took the time to reread it. What a rich experience! This time through I already knew the plot, so I was able to more fully realize Hugo's genius in showing us character transformation.

Taking time to read literature and meet for Well-Read Mom isn't always convenient. Good intentions are not enough. It involves a decision. It takes time. It requires effort. But the fruit of this effort is a great reward: a growing capacity for attentiveness, increased empathy, and a focused vision that sees a deeper dimension in life.

Attentiveness, empathy, and vision, in turn, help us develop a greater capacity for relationships. Friends help us in this habit of reading, and the habit of reading helps us in friendship.

Meaningful Conversation Leads to Meaningful Connection

In her book *Reclaiming Conversation*, Sherry Turkle says, "Face-to-face conversation is the most human—and humanizing—thing we do. Fully present to one another, we learn to listen. It's where we develop the capacity for empathy. It's where we experience the joy of being heard, of being understood."

But this level of conversation can be hard to come by. Often we get stuck at the level of small talk, exchanging updates about our kids or recipes or shopping finds. Chatting can be fun, but for me, it's not enough. My heart is nourished when I hear people's stories and share my story, and when we step back to look at our lives as part of a much bigger story.

Books—especially *good* books—provide an ideal springboard for diving into deeper conversations. Chats about the characters and their experiences open doors for us to consider our own experiences in a new light or to explore questions we've long wondered about—in the safety of a cozy living room with like-minded people. (And if the others in the group turn out not to be like-minded, so much the better. Developing friendships with people who are different expands our horizons.)

A stimulating conversation has to be about something. It needs a center, a focus, an idea. Taking part in a conversation requires us to process ideas. We need to think, to focus our attention.

"Reclaiming conversation begins with reclaiming our attention," Sherry Turkle notes. Reading prepares us for deeper conversation because it offers space for self-reflection, for ideas to take root. In this sense, reading helps us become better conversationalists. And conversing about literature makes us better readers.

Friendship with the Author

There is a pleasure when we read and realize the author is sharing something we recognize to be true. I often read something and think,

Yes! That's exactly right! That's what I feel or think, but I couldn't have put it into words like that! I was amazed, for example, by Wendell Berry's description, in his novel *Hannah Coulter*, of nursing a newborn.

> I took her into bed with me and propped myself up with pillows against the headboard to let her nurse. As she nursed and the milk came, she began a little low contented sort of singing. I would feel milk and love flowing from me to her as once it had flowed to me. It emptied me. As the baby fed, I seemed slowly to grow empty of myself, as if in the presence of that long flow of love even grief could not stand.

Later in the book there is this incredible description of a mother's love for her grown child:

> I have this love for Mattie. It was formed in me as he himself was formed. It has his shape, you might say. He fits it. He fits into it as he fits into his clothes. He will always fit into it. When he gets out of the car and I meet him and hug him, there he is, him himself, something of my very own forever, and my love for him goes all around him just as it did when he was a baby and a little boy and a young man grown.

Walker Percy talks about the reader's recognition—sometimes the shock of recognition—that comes from reading something we knew but didn't realize we knew. When this happens, we have a sense that we are not alone. We are deeply connected to others by our common humanity. We share our humanity with the author, the characters, and most of all, the other people in the room who just read the same book.

Each of us is unique. At the same time, we all share our essential humanity. It is a joy to discover not only the details of our experiences that are unique but also the ones we share. Talking about books provides an ideal platform for this type of conversation.

So much good happens through friendship. When women meet with other women, we don't really know where the conversation will wind up, but it is safe to begin talking about the novel, and then doors open to talk about life.

Staying Together Sets Up for Success

If a train does not have tracks to roll on, it is nearly impossible for that locomotive to travel far. Laying down tracks makes it easier for the train to start rolling. Even though it still takes an effort, once that locomotive gets moving, the tracks provide direction and ease the friction as the train speeds along to its destination.

An established book group can be like train tracks to make reaching the destination of becoming well-read easier, more enjoyable, and more life-giving. Yes, it still takes personal effort, but being part of a well-thought-through program provides the itinerary for the adventure. You just get on board.

When my boys were in high school and training for cross-country, they would log hundreds of miles every season. Why? Not because they loved to run. It was simply because they were on the team. The coach made out the training schedule, and because the boys wanted to be with their friends on the team, they followed what was asked. As the months went by, they became serious runners—at least during cross country season.

That's how friendship impacts reading. A woman may join a group to be with friends and then find herself following along. Maybe she only reads a couple of chapters from a book at first. As time passes, she might begin to realize she is not only reading more but also enjoying it. She is not afraid of tackling a book that might have intimidated her before. Now she's an insider in the literary world.

Women from many different backgrounds, some who were once more comfortable with scientific journals, marketing analyses, or mathematical reports—and not sure that literature was their "thing"—have discovered that fiction is approachable. One of the women in my group is a physician. When she joined, she said, "I'm not really a reader. It's all I can do to keep up with medical journals. I can't remember the last novel I read." That was seven years ago. Now she confidently refers to herself as a reader, and she has found time to read almost all the books. Being part of the group month by month, year by year, has transformed her into a serious reader.

For me personally, Well-Read Mom is sometimes an overwhelming endeavor. There's so much to tend to! The mission is so big. Yet every month at our gathering, I find myself surprised again by the quality of the conversation, the bond of friendship, the opening of my own heart. I walk away grateful.

Part Two
Why Reading Matters
for Women

"Unless we regain the art of silence and insight, the ability for non-activity, unless we substitute true leisure for our hectic amusements, we will destroy our culture — and ourselves."

—from the cover of *Leisure as the Basis of Culture*,
Joseph Pieper

"Women need to receive and receive greatly."

—Elizabeth M. Kelly

Chapter 3

Reading is a Form of Self-Care

PUTTING OURSELVES AT THE BOTTOM OF THE PRIORITY LIST

One of Aesop's fables is about a goose who lays, each day, a golden egg. Her owners, thinking she must have pure gold inside her, greedily cut her open. They discover an ordinary goose, but alas, a dead one. Now their supply of golden eggs is gone.

The main moral of the story is clear: be grateful for the good you receive, and don't demand so much that it destroys the source of that goodness. But perhaps there is another lesson from this fable, if looked at from the goose's perspective. Imagine if the goose had been an overly generous goose. Seeing that people needed her eggs, she might have driven herself to produce more and more—to the point of sickness or death. She may have even offered herself as a martyr, thinking that her family would benefit from whatever it was inside her producing those eggs. But alas—it was her life and her health that produced the eggs. The noblest thing she could have done would have been to stay healthy and to thrive so that she could continue to give her precious gifts of golden eggs.

The good we do for the people around us springs from the life inside us. To nourish that life is to maintain the ability to give our best.

Many women hold a deep (perhaps subconscious) belief that self-care is selfish. They conclude that it's okay to take care of themselves if—and only if—everyone else's needs are met. This belief is illogical. A woman spiraling in this direction is in danger of being depleted. And a depleted soul has little to give anyone. This type of unbalanced martyrdom ends up actually hurting the people we love because we destroy our own capacity to serve them. I know this from experience.

BURNOUT

I remember locking myself in my bedroom one day to escape from the children and be alone to think for a few minutes. Not more than two minutes went by before my eight-year-old was pounding on the door asking why it was locked. "Nick, I just need to be alone for a few minutes."

"OK," he said, "but do you think I could still ask you something while you're in there?"

"What?"

"Well, I'm just wondering, Mom, what are we going to do about all these trees being cut down in the rainforest?"

"Not now, Nick. We'll talk about this later."

Frazzled, I lay on the bed and stared at the ceiling in the darkening room. *Does anyone in this family see that I can't keep going like this? I love being a mom. I know I'm needed and loved, but somehow, the real me seems to be invisible to everyone. The kids don't seem to see that I have needs, too.* I continued to stare, praying for the grace to get up and face the next shift: the dinner hour.

When does a mother rest? A family's needs are constant.

"Mom, I'm so hungry. Is supper ready yet?" one child would ask minutes after we returned home from an all-day sporting event. Frustrated, I wondered why he couldn't see that he and I had gotten home at the same time. How *could* dinner be ready?

There is no margin for moms. Sighing, I wondered how I could I keep pace with the constant demands.

A REVOLUTIONARY CHANGE IN MY THINKING

Not long after that, when I was driving to my son John's cross country meet, I stopped at a coffee shop and ordered a large latte. In the coffee shop, I stared at the wall. *If I don't get going, I'm going to miss John's meet.* I realized this but continued to sit. I continued to stare. I didn't get up. I missed the meet. What was wrong with me?

A couple of weeks later, I told my friend Elisabetta about this in-cident. What she said would bring about a revolutionary change in my understanding of motherhood. "Do you think that being a mom is all about running to everything your kids are in? Take care of your heart! That's how you mother!" Her words struck like a knife. They hurt, but I intuited that they were true. She was saying something directly to me, and I needed to pay attention. Her words were new. I had never heard this before. What did it mean to take care of my heart?

THE HEART OF MOTHERING

"Take care of your heart, that's how you mother." What a strange correction. Elisabetta's words stung, but they continued to echo. She is my friend. She doesn't just commiserate; she tells me what she sees. Having moved to America from Italy, she saw my life through a differ-ent cultural lens.

"Look, if your kids want to run, let them run. If they want to play tennis, let them play tennis. But to mother, take care of your heart."

I had to think about this. What did taking care of my heart have to do with being a wife and mother? What would it even look like?

It seems obvious to me now, but at the time it was a real question. I thought I was fully embracing motherhood. I was a hands-on mom, super involved. *If I do take care of my heart in a new way*, I wondered, *how will that change my experience of being a mom?*

THE MECHANICAL MOM

When Beth was 12, I remember being in a rush to get her to ballet lessons. In Minnesota, everything takes longer in the winter, especially getting out the door. After zipping two toddlers into snowsuits, I dug through the closet looking for a missing boot. "Oh, and where are those library books?"

Finally, everyone was buckled in the big green van, and we were off. My mind buzzed with the list of errands I would run while Beth was at ballet. When I pulled up to the dance studio with two minutes to spare, I have to admit feeling rather proud.

"Okay, Beth, have a good lesson. We'll see you in an hour. Hurry up, get in there so you won't be late."

Silence in the van.

"Beth?"

No answer. No Beth.

In the hustle of managing details, I had left my daughter behind. In taking care of the tasks, I had left the person behind.

This is our danger as women. This is what Elisabetta was talking about. The problem was not the activities. The problem was that I was living like a top spinning out of control. I was giving my attention and focus to the activities—to the periphery of life—and neglecting my own center. I was carrying on in a robotic way, and my own person (not to mention the personhood of my children) was getting left behind.

When life becomes a kind of *doing* that lacks a sense of the mystery of *being*, we are not able to be *present* to our children in as true a way.

Taking care of my heart, I was beginning to see, had something to do with taking the inner journey seriously, and this had something to do with not leaving my own person behind.

DON'T FORGET TO INCLUDE YOURSELF

I have an exceptional mother-in-law. Peg has loved me and wanted the best for me from the moment I met her. Once, when she came to visit, she saw my worn-out state. "A family is a circle of love," she told me. "Everyone's needs are looked after in this circle of love." Then she looked me in the eyes and held my hands. "Don't forget to include yourself in the circle."

Everyone needs to flourish in the family. A mother is part of the family and needs to flourish, too. It seems obvious, but in practice, many women neglect their own legitimate needs. We are givers. We are born to give. This is good and beautiful if we maintain access to the continual Source that fills us. Giving and receiving is a beautiful way to live. Reconnecting to the Source is the goal of self-care.

HELPING THE FAMILY TO THRIVE

Sometimes we think we're doing what's best for the family when we leave ourselves behind and neglect our real needs. But we as mothers are an essential part of the fabric of the family, so if we start to unravel, this threatens the integrity of the whole fabric.

My friend Liz Kelly teaches a course at the University of St. Thomas called Woman and Man. She told me that she asks students, "What is the center of the family? What's the focus of the family?" Students typically answer, "the children."

She explains, "The *family* is the focus of the family. It's the entire unit. Everyone in it needs to be flourishing. Of course, children take a certain kind of primacy, because they are unable to care for themselves, but they are not to be exalted above the parents. The family needs to take care of the family, the whole unit."

A child has eternal value. Whether or not he plays the violin or soccer is a secondary, even tertiary issue. The primary question is, how are we doing as a family? Is there room for a particular activity to be added in? This discernment is necessary so that we are not living an unessential busyness.

Constant activity leads to burnout, and burnout is real. When we are doing things that aren't essential or even doing things that are essential but without an ordered rhythm for restoration and rest, our person can be left behind.

My daughter Beth is now the mother of four young children, and she recently wrote about the same concept in a slightly different way:

> There is a certain mentality out there: "I do all these things for my kids, and everything is about the kids." I think of it a little differently because our life is not all about the kids being in activities. It is about something much bigger. When we were growing up, my dad would tell my mom, "If it is good for the family, then it is good for that particular kid." So if it is good for the family, it is good for my daughter, it is good for my son. So, if I am losing myself by having to run the kids to different things, the dance class would not actually be good for them. I have to recover myself somehow: make time to pray, or go to Mass sometimes, or read a novel. I have to recover myself so that it is good for the whole family.

It's easy to understand the needs of a two-year-old who is having a meltdown after a day of errands with his mom who is on the go. The mother looks at her child and realizes, "My little guy has missed his nap. He's had too much candy and too much stimulation." The mother understands that the child is not just being naughty. He has real needs. The child needs to eat some satisfying food, take a bath, be cuddled, read to, prayed with, and tucked into bed. He needs to be reoriented home.

Overload is easy to see with children, but with ourselves, it is more difficult to recognize.

To keep charging ahead on the same path, maybe eliminating an activity or two, will not bring about the needed change.

When Virgil acted as Dante's guide, he instructed, "Thee it behooves to take another road." Taking another road in the area of self-care may not be popular, and we may resist it at first. On this new road the giving comes from a place of receiving. There is an awareness of our need to receive: in prayer, in listening, in reading, in a quietness of heart. These are the things that reorient us home.

LEGITIMATE SELF-CARE

Of course self-care needs to start with the essentials for survival: sufficient sleep, nutritious food, some sort of exercise, enough order in the home for the family to function. These are essential needs, but there is another level of self-care that includes investing in our long-term growth as human beings and children of God; it involves feeding our minds and our souls.

READING AS SELF-CARE

When I was a young mother in a book club for the first time, I realized I was participating in something that was helping me grow as a person. After we moved, reading the classics faded out of my routine. With precious little free time, I felt guilty about taking the time to read a novel. I hate to admit it, but reading felt like a waste of time. Yet that early positive experience was a clue for me that reading was a source of life for my soul.

Today, reading is a regular part of my life that I treasure. But I do have to intentionally guard it. No one in the family is going to make sure that I take time each week to read. My failure to be a faithful reader won't cause anyone in my family to panic—at least not the way they might panic if there weren't groceries in the fridge.

In the short term, my not reading could easily go unnoticed by everyone. Just like no one would really notice if I neglected to plant tomatoes and onions in our garden in the spring. But if I do the hidden work of planting seeds in spring, I'll later reap a harvest that will bless my family and even some neighbors. In a similar way, if I do the hidden work of receiving good ideas and stories and insights and words, my mind becomes a fruitful garden that can bless the people around me with meaningful conversations and a deeper, broader perspective on life.

Investing in my own growth and development this week—even though it doesn't feel urgent—will bear fruit in years to come. That fruit might take the form of deep, significant conversations with teenagers and adult children. It is not *against* our families when we work to fit reading into our schedule, it is *for* them. Meaningful mothering down the road comes from intentional living now.

TAKING CARE OF YOUR MIND

"Being a stay at home mom can be an intellectual hazard," a friend of mine sighed. She is right. But it is not just mothers at home who have to fight to give space to the life of the mind. It is a challenge for every single person.

American culture in the twenty-first century does not value the life of the intellect in the way that it may have in the past. Today, our attention is more often captured by shows to entertain, products to purchase, and smart phones to scan rather than the pleasures that come from careful thinking and disciplined reflection.

Servant of God Elisabeth Leseur wrote this in her diary: "It is a duty to develop unceasingly one's intelligence, to strengthen one's character, to become a creature of thought and will; it is a duty to view life with joy and face it with energy. Finally, it is a duty to be able to understand one's time and not despair of the future. All this a woman can do." Elisabeth understood the value of this discipline when she wrote, "Every soul that raises itself raises the world."

Time to read and study is not a vacation from real life, instead it is nourishment to help us live life with greater fullness and wisdom. Read to embrace, not run, from your vocation. Read to be a good steward of the mind God has given you.

There are important biochemical reasons to keep reading—reading is physiologically good for you. Reading keeps our brains alert and active, which slows the cognitive decline as we get older. Reading improves vocabulary, reasoning ability, empathy, social perception, and emotional intelligence. Researchers from Yale School of Public Health showed that reading a book for 30 minutes a day can add two years to a person's life span. Questioning over 3,500 people over the age of 50 from different backgrounds, they found that book readers had a 20 percent lower chance of dying over the following 12 years compared with those who read magazines and newspapers or didn't read at all.

How does reading keep our brains healthy? According to Maryanne Wolf, in her book *Proust and the Squid: The Story and Science of the Reading Brain*, when we read, "we are forced to construct, to produce narrative, to imagine. Typically, when you read, you have more time to think. Reading gives you a unique pause button for comprehension and insight. By and large, with oral language—when you watch a film or listen to a tape—you don't press pause" to stop and really ponder an issue. Sitting with a book, however, invites this type of contemplation. It's true that listening to audiobooks provides more work for your brain than seeing a movie—but reading from print should take up part of our lives too. A literate mind is a more complex one. "There's a richness that reading gives you," Wolf says, "an opportunity to probe more than any other medium I know of."

TOWARDS A DEEPER UNDERSTANDING OF LEISURE

At the start of Well-Read Mom, when I picked up St. Pope John Paul II's "Letter to Women," I was shocked. He writes, "Women will increasingly play a part in solving the serious problems of the future." That didn't surprise me; surely women will play a part in solving serious problems. What did surprise me was the first serious problem listed that women would help solve. It was "leisure time."

Leisure time? How is leisure time a problem? When I think about the vast array of pressing, complex social issues, leisure is not even on my radar. In fact, leisure was not something I had thought much about at all. How could it be a serious problem that women would help solve?

At that moment, I realized that either Pope John Paul II was confused or I didn't understand the word *leisure*. He had me curious. Something about the nature of leisure must have something to do with our humanity. And that something must be in jeopardy in the modern world.

Continuing the letter, I was surprised again by the second serious problem listed that women would help solve: "quality of life." Perhaps there was a connection. Could it be that leisure has something to do with quality of life? Could spending leisure time in an intentional way affect the quality of not only a woman's life but also the family's life and society?

A few weeks later, my son Nick came home from college and plopped a stack of books down on the kitchen counter. "Mom, here's a book you've got to read," he said handing me *Leisure: the Basis of Culture*, by Josef Pieper. I was startled. There was that word again: *leisure*. And Pieper was calling leisure the basis of culture! *This must be what John Paul was referring to.* As I read Pieper, I understood that this master philosopher was introducing me to a life-changing definition and understanding of leisure.

Leisure is not entertainment or amusement, as I had naively assumed. Up until this time, I thought it meant having time off to do what I wanted—which, at that time included escaping for a few hours to get away from my reality of being at home with small children. I'd look forward to these getaways to chit-chat with girlfriends, shop, or to go to a movie. These things were fun; they still are—I'm not recommending anyone give them up! But they weren't restoring my soul. I needed more.

"Leisure," says Pieper, "is a mental and spiritual attitude that fosters a capacity to perceive the reality of the world. . . . It is not the inevitable result of spare time, a holiday, a weekend or a vacation." The mere fact that I go for a walk in the woods won't restore my soul if I'm not open to seeing and hearing God. "Leisure," Pieper continues, "is a receptive attitude of mind, a contemplative attitude, and it is not only the occasion but also the capacity for steeping oneself in the whole of creation." Leisure is the way we reconnect to God and the big picture of creation, life, and love—the things that really matter.

Pieper calls true leisure an "engaging work." I wasn't thrilled with this paradox of leisure being work. With the busy family life that seven children bring, the last thing I was looking for was more work—even if it was "engaging." It seemed counter-intuitive. But because I was on the verge of serious burnout yet again, I paid attention. *Could it be that this insight on the nature of leisure is an answer to my need?*

This is why reading Pieper was revolutionary. I came to understand that what I needed most was to engage in something that restored me, and literature did just that.

Suddenly, reading was not just one more way to distract myself from my duties; in a sense, it was a duty. Leisure helps me become my best self, which blesses my family and society. I did not need to apologize or feel guilty about reading. (Obviously, anything can be taken to an extreme, but that's not what was going on.) Pieper's insight pointed me toward edifying, high quality literature, the stories that would help me grow in understanding life and my journey through it.

IN NOT WANTING TO MISS OUT, WE MISSED OUT

How can our eyes be trained to see with the awareness of the Psalmist who cried out, "The heavens are telling the glory of God"?

In a WRM podcast, last year, Sister Veronica from Sisters of Life described taking a group of women to watch the sunrise. On the way to the lookout, the women chatted. When the sun peeked over the hill, the picture-taking began. Then, with the sun behind them, they took more pictures of each other and the group. No one wanted to miss anything.

The next day sister proposed watching the sunrise again, but this time in a different way. She asked them to keep silent and notice things like a breeze, the field of corn on the left, the moving clouds. This time, sitting at the lookout, they watched. They waited. They listened. And the sun came up.

Following this silent hike, one woman wrote a poem, another painted a picture, and another woman took time to journal. All the women continued  to ponder the experience. The waiting and watching became a time of receiving and seeing. It was a restorative experience of beauty that stirred tears, thoughts, reflections, and creativity.

An Experience of Restorative Leisure

My friend Janel was listening to an audio recording of *Middlemarch* while folding clothes, and she realized that she wasn't even following the story. It was a frustrating experience. So she decided to go outside and lie on the trampoline for a few minutes, listening to the story while watching the clouds. "It was a completely different experience," she said, "it was restorative!"

I'm not suggesting that there's anything wrong with listening to an audiobook while we do other things, but if we find ourselves not experiencing enjoyment, it may be a sign that multitasking is not working. The goal is to be refreshed.

Reading: A Waste of Time?

Do I really have time to read books like Gaudy Night *and Dante's* Divine Comedy*? you wonder. What if reading these novels is a waste of time?*

Could it be that it is the wrong "waste of time" we fear? What if living in a frenetic state of busyness is the real time-waster, and Dante is the gold, awakening us to the true journey of life?

Admitting Our Need, Joining Forces

A commitment to bring back leisure comes from an awareness of need. When a person is without water in the desert, she experiences thirst. Water becomes her single desire. But if that person drinks coffee or soda all day long, she may not realize her need for water.

We do not live in a cultural desert. Quite the opposite. We have places to go, errands to run, people who need us, and countless activities to distract us. The need for pure refreshment is not apparent.

It's easy to lose touch with the cry of our own souls. One woman told me, "I do so much for everyone else, I honestly don't know what I enjoy anymore."

Women need to give themselves permission: permission to read, to rest, to experience leisure, and to grow in interiority. Yes, all this a woman can do if she is intentional and accompanied along the way.

Pope John Paul II's "Letter to Women" led me to understand that bringing leisure back into our society is a particular call women can pursue together. The impact is not just personal. It ripples out to our families and friends, and into the culture. But it all starts with feeding our own souls.

"If mama ain't happy, ain't nobody happy."

—Anonymous

"Give less attention to the problem and more attention to the business of living fully. Nothing is so compelling to encourage others toward rational living as the presence of a vibrant, healthy force in the home. As you turn your attention away from the problem and toward strengthening yourself in body, mind, and spirit, you may be surprised at the influence you have."

—Sarah Felton, *When You Live with a Messie*

Chapter 4

Reading Brings Parenting Wisdom

One fruit of being a reader is that we are more tuned in to books and stories. We become more likely to read to our children, which can have immeasurable benefits for their formation. A child who is read to is exposed to thousands of words, and this leads to rich language development. More importantly, reading to our children can shape their moral imaginations and enable them to visualize virtues.

Another fruit of personal reading is the wisdom and self-understanding we gain. As moms, we need insight so we can make choices that benefit our families.

We can also gain strength and encouragement from the characters we come to know in great books. We learn we are not alone. Others mothers have gone before us. They have faced and overcome difficulties raising their children, difficulties in marriage, difficulty in balancing all the demands of adult life. We can, too.

Not only that, but as we take time for our own reading, we model an intentional and well-ordered way of living. Intentional living brings peace to the household. As our children grow and establish their own homes and families, their positive experiences of growing up in a home where reading is a priority will stand them in good stead. Children who see their parents reading are more likely to become lifelong readers themselves.

GOOD STORIES MAKE GOOD LESSONS

When my daughter Margaret was six, she wanted to get in on the intense basketball game going on in our driveway. So she took charge and commanded her brothers: "Mom says you have to let me play, or you'll be in trouble."

Johnnie came running into the kitchen where I was making dinner, "Mom, do we have to let Margaret play? She said you said we had to let her in. We're in the middle of a really good game!"

"No, you guys keep playing. I didn't tell Margaret that," I let him know.

When the scenario happened again, Philip challenged me: "Mom, Margaret is lying; you should do something about this!"

Sigh! Discipline is never convenient. Taking her by the hand, I led little Marg to the couch, pulled William Bennett's *Book of Virtues* from the shelf and paged to the Aesop's fable of "The Boy Who Cried Wolf." Without nagging or scolding or raising my voice, I read. She listened. Her imagination came into play. Margaret began to get a glimmer of insight. The boy cried "Wolf!" because he wanted attention; he wanted to belong. She lied because she wanted attention; she wanted to belong.

In a concrete but non-confrontational way, this story helped to reach Margaret's heart. As parents, we learn that coercing our kids doesn't work. We need to reach our children's hearts. Without my having to command or force, Margaret saw that lying was not getting her what she wanted. "The Boy Who Cried Wolf" engaged and enlarged her mind and heart.

C. S. Lewis argued that while reason is the natural organ of truth, "imagination is the organ of meaning." We often do not grasp the meaning of a command or principle until we have a clear image to help us picture the command. Imagination helps us grasp meaning. This is why stories can help us comprehend truths: they help us picture them. Margaret may not have grasped this concept instantly, but I could see that she grasped something that day. Over time, these images from stories help support the virtues we hope to pass on to our children because they become patterns and then habits that help shape our way of thinking about the world we live in and about right and wrong.

In raising seven children, my husband Pete and I found reading stories to our children to be not only enjoyable but also helpful to educate imaginations (ours as well as the children's) in a way that continues to help us move toward what is good and beautiful and true.

STORIES HELP CHILDREN SEE WHO THEY CAN BECOME

When Philip was nine, he came into the kitchen perplexed. "Mom I just don't know what I'm going to be when I grow up."

"What are you thinking?" I was curious.

"I don't know, either a priest, maybe a king, or else a professional golfer." At that time, I was reading *The Lion, the Witch and the Wardrobe* to the kids. In the enchanted world of Narnia, Peter, Lucy, Susan, and Edmund actually do become kings and queens. Yes, it is just a story, but one that resonates deeply. Through it, we glimpse imaginative realities that show us, surprisingly, exactly who we are. As the Pevensie children follow Aslan and are crowned kings and queens of Narnia, we understand that like them, we too are made for greatness, that we are also sons and daughters of the King. But if, instead of vicariously experiencing this, our kids are simply told "You're a prince," or "You're a princess," the words don't have the same impact. Listening to *The Lion, the Witch and the Wardrobe* helps form a deep connection. We somehow know, "It's true! This is exactly who I am!" This is how good fantasy writing can function as a window into truth.

Realistic fiction can work the same way, inviting our imagination to form a picture of goodness. In just one sentence from one of the *Little House on the Prairie* books, you can imagine a way of life: "Laura and Mary finished their bowl of mush with prairie-hen gravy, and hurried to help Ma wash the dishes." That simple sentence awakens me to a positive example of family life. In the Ingalls family, Laura and Mary helped Ma. They were prompt and considerate. Without complaining, they pitched in. My desire is kindled, I want to run help Ma wash the dishes, too! Over time, a steady flow of these images becomes a new pattern of thinking and then a habit that moves us toward what is good and true.

Telling children the difference between right and wrong is good. Showing them is better. Capturing their imaginations with a compelling story of what virtue looks like is better still—because it inspires them from within. Robert Houston Smith writes, "When functioning as it should . . . imagination is the most important means by which higher truths can be communicated." Conscience speaks to conscience through great literature.

STORIES CAN HELP US PERSEVERE

Parenting is some of the most important work in the world—and some of the hardest! It's normal for us to feel spent and weary even after a good day with kids!

Reading can be a source of encouragement on the journey. Again and again, I've been strengthened as a mother through reading. Every day I read from the greatest book, the Bible, for sustenance and truth. There is no book that could ever replace the Sacred Scriptures. But other books can spark encouragement in sometimes surprising ways as well.

Maybe you are isolated from other adults, feeling weighed down at home with small children at your heels. Maybe you wonder if what you are doing is really that important. Could the thousands of actions every day—wiping little noses and putting shoes on little feet—really be part of something bigger for all eternity? Yes! But it is sometimes hard to see that serving a little person is some of the most important work in the world. Books can remind us of our part in the bigger story.

The way we live our days matters. Holy things can be happening unnoticed within ordinary routines of a mother's day. I realized this again when I read a text written nearly a hundred years ago about a simple incident in the life of Mrs. Barrett, a stay-at-home mom, who had an impact on the neighbor girl:

> It was Mrs. Barrett who gave me my first impulse towards Catholicism. It was around ten o'clock in the morning that I went up to Kathryn's to call for her to come out and play. ... In the front bedroom, Mrs. Barrett was on her knees, saying her prayers. She turned to tell me that Kathryn and the children had all gone to the store and went on with her praying, and I felt a warm burst of love toward Mrs. Barrett that I have never forgotten, a feeling of gratitude and happiness that still warms my heart when I remember her. She had God, and there was beauty and joy in her life. All through my life what she was doing remained with me. Mrs. Barrett in her sordid little tenement flat finished her breakfast dishes at ten o'clock in the morning and got down on her knees and prayed to God.

Mrs. Barrett, an ordinary mom, was doing her duty and seeking her God. What Mrs. Barrett didn't know at the time was that by being faithful to her work and her prayers in her tenement flat, she would have something to do with the conversion of a modern-day saint; the little girl at the door was Dorothy Day.

And almost 100 years later, reading about the life of Mrs. Barrett from Dorothy's autobiography, *The Long Loneliness*, I realize that the way I live my life in the small circle of my family and neighbors can make a difference. Mrs. Barrett encourages me to persevere.

Dr. Louise Cowan writes, "The spark that kindles the imagination in one can catch fire in another." Someone else's words, whether we read them in a book or listen to them around a table, can inspire us with courage and a will to emulate the good.

When Moms Read More, Kids Read More

Many parents realize the importance of reading to children or having them read on their own at least 20 minutes per day. (Many school districts recommend 20 minutes of reading to keep kids on grade level.)

If you tell your children to read but don't take time to read for yourself, what does that communicate? Maybe they'll conclude that reading is something kids have to do for school, and as soon as they are out of school, they'll be free of reading, as free as their parents.

But if you treasure and protect your own reading time, if you excitedly share quotes or relay little stories or scenes from your book with the family over dinner, if you look forward to your book discussion group—then it's possible that your kids will catch your love of reading.

I remember the day I walked over to my good friend Teri's house. Poking my head in the door, I saw a disaster: the sink and counters piled with dishes, the laundry room overflowing with piles of laundry. There was Teri, lying on the couch reading the gigantic novel *Kristin Lavransdatter*. "This is your fault!" she hollered over to me, smiling.

"What's my fault?" I asked.

"Look at this place; it's a mess. You gave me this book, and now I can't put it down." Of course, Teri eventually got her house in order. But for a week, maybe two, she took time to read this great book, and that meant leaving some things undone.

Fast forward fifteen years. Her little ones are now college students. On a summer day in June, there's a knock on my door. It is Teri's son Coltan: "Marcie, I was just wondering if I could use your deck to read some books this summer. There's so much activity at our house I can't concentrate."

There he stood with a pile of books. I was thrilled to see Coltan sitting in the lawn chair reading C. S. Lewis and other great authors that summer. It confirmed for me that when Teri took time to read, even when other things were temporarily left undone, she was modeling something precious. Children who see Mom reading for pleasure quickly get the message that reading is a pleasure. When you've passed on a love of reading to your kids, you've done something right as a parent. As far as I know, all seven of Teri and John's kids are readers. The parents' reading became a tremendous gift for their children. By taking their own hearts seriously, they did some of their best parenting.

PARENTING WITH CONFIDENCE

Is it possible for a mother to have some quiet time to think and read daily? It may be possible, but it takes some strategizing to make reading a priority in daily life. How do mothers do it? While I offer some detailed, practical strategies in Part 3 of this book, here I want to talk about a principle that helped me improve not only my approach to parenting but also the way I organized my days. I've learned a great deal through trial and error. Though it may sound strange to you, the principle is to parent with greater certainty.

Other women have come to the same insight.

My daughter asked her friend how his mother raised 10 children and was surprised by his response: "She had a certainty of what we needed." His mother was certain about her authority. She was certain that her kids would get along in life if they learned to obey and work and eat regular meals, get plenty of play outside, and so on. In short, she understood her role as mother.

What I see today is that mothers lack confidence. We question what is best for our children and what they need, wrestling with continual doubts. Endless "experts" post articles about how to raise children. And so a mom questions herself:

- Am I doing the right thing as a parent?
- How should I handle this situation?
- How do I discipline them?
- Should I be playing more with my kids?
- Why do they resist me so much?
- Wouldn't it be easier to do the chores myself than to face a fight?

As a mom, I realized that when it came to disciplining my kids, I was a softie. I would constantly give in to their requests. Give and take is good in some situations, but when it becomes a way of living, it stifles my child's ability to grow in taking responsibility. It also gets in the way of my need for some relaxation. It becomes a problem.

One particular day, I had just had it. I was reading a novel to my children, and no one was appreciating it. Paper airplanes were flying. Kids were fighting. I threw the book down exploding, "That's it!" Then I did what I was in the habit of doing in times of out-of-control chaos: I locked myself in the bathroom. Realizing their disobedience, the kids quietly stood at the door asking for forgiveness. "Mom, we're sorry we were bad. Can we have another chance? We will be better, we promise. Please can you read to us again?"

No answer. Still shaken up, I stayed in the locked room.

"No, I'm not coming out," was my reply (which I realize was an immature response, but I was at my wits' end). Something was out of order. My kids were not obeying me, and I was frazzled. Something had to change.

Later that afternoon I sought out a wise grandmother. Mary spoke words of truth about parenting to my soul. It was like I was hearing these truths for the first time.

"You are the mom," she started out. "You only need to say something one time, and your children need to obey."

"I agree with you, Mary, but that's just not how it works: I say something and then I say it again and I get louder. They don't obey."

Again, she reiterated, "You are the mom! God has given you authority. You don't need to raise your voice, or repeat commands over and over. You have the authority. They will obey."

She continued, "Your words matter. If you ask something, you must be ready to follow through each and every time with a consequence, or else don't ask it."

It all sounded so easy the way she told it, but every mom knows it isn't. Still, as she explained these truths, I felt my heart and mind opening to receive.

Her counsel helped me envision my role as a parent in a new way. "You are the Mom," she said, "and you've been given this authority, so be parental." As I drove home in my big van, I found myself filling with a confident joy. I gave thanks to God as I sped down the freeway chanting, "I am the Mom! They will obey!"

When I returned home, the kids were still gun-shy from the earlier fiasco.

"Kids, gather around. I've made a discovery." They were curious.

"I apologize for my explosion today. I was wrong. Will you forgive me?" I looked at each child. They nodded their heads up and down.

"I've discovered something that is going to be a big help in our family."

What could it be? they wondered.

"I've discovered that I am the mom!"

At this point they eyed each other. *Is mom okay? You mean she didn't know this before?*

But I was okay. That was the day I began to mother in a new way. The nagging and threats stopped. I was careful to speak in a normal tone. I stopped raising my voice. I followed through. I saw that my words and actions mattered. I saw that in order to lead my children, I needed to live with integrity in words and actions. Eventually, greater order and peace came into the home, which was a blessing for the whole family. And with it, there came more free time for me.

Here's a scenario from a couple years ago when I *did* parent with certainty, and it allowed me to keep reading:

"Mom, can I go over to the coffee shop with Maddie and Teresa?" fourteen-year-old Emma asks.

I look up from my reading, "Is your room clean? Is the dishwasher unloaded and loaded?"

"Uh . . . well no . . . but I could get it done when I get home because they are waiting for me."

Silence. I calmly go back to my reading.

I hear Emma sprinting upstairs to clean her room. Soon I hear shuffling in the kitchen as she hurries to finish her chores.

Ten minutes later: "Okay, Mom, can I go now? Everything is done."

"Sure, have a great time, honey! Call me when you are on your way home."

No stress for me. No whining. No begging from my teenager. I keep reading. Everyone understands that unless there is an emergency, chores need to be done, or they don't go out.

Now what would have happened if I had lacked certainty as a parent and had given in to the request?

Emma, who had not unloaded and loaded the dishwasher, would have gone off with her friends. I would have realized that before I could get dinner going, I would need to do Emma's undone chores in the kitchen. I would quit reading. My daughter would be with her friends, and I'd be doing her work.

Often we are softies as moms because we don't want our kids to "miss out" or be disappointed. We lack certainty of what is best for our kids.

I remember one of my boys challenging me saying, "But I do so much work around here! What does Dad even do for chores?"

"Yes, you help out, and I appreciate that," I acknowledged, "but let's look at what Dad is doing today. He got up at six and had a seven o'clock conference call. Then he loaded up tires in the truck before work to drop off at the Tire Center so we can get snow tires on our cars for winter. He went to work for 10 hours, probably worked though his lunch hour, and finished in time to pick you up from practice on his way home. Just now, he helped me carry in groceries. So please take the garbage and recycling out without complaining."

That put things in perspective!

It is okay for kids to be miserable sometimes. Chores teach kids that life doesn't revolve around them. They are part of what makes us stay together in a more beautiful way as a family. Mothers are part of the family, too. When everyone pitches in, it helps us live together more peacefully. My parents used to stress the importance of learning how to work. "Hard work never hurt anyone" was their mantra. It is good for children to do their part in the home. It is preparation for the responsibilities in life.

It is good for the kids to suffer some natural and fair consequences as a result of their behavior. Because we often waver and give in, our own legitimate needs are compromised. Many moms unnecessarily drain themselves of needed energy because they don't really believe they know what's best for their children It is exhausting to question every decision as a mom!

Parenting is more than finding the right techniques. It has to do with a deeper understanding of who we are as mothers and fathers.

Parenting requires swimming upstream. Stay strong. Some day your kids will thank you, though that some day may take 20 years. Parenting with certainty can help us create an environment that works for everyone in the family's development and happiness.

RUNNING OUR HOMES

"Mom I can't study in our house. It's too messy. I need to go to the coffee shop."

"Really?" I was surprised, but as I looked around the kitchen and laundry room, Emma was right. Disorder reigned. With piles of papers here and piles of laundry there, disarray and confusion loomed everywhere! Every cabinet and drawer was overflowing.

That evening I headed to my Well-Read Mom discussion of *The Seven Storey Mountain*. Jill shared her surprise at Thomas Merton's all-in obedience when he was asked to do mundane tasks in the monastery. As she shared, I understood something about my all-out avoidance of certain necessary-but-mundane tasks that would maintain more order in my home.

My home management dilemma was not a consequence of poor organizing skills. The problem went deeper. I was running from my vocation. *Surely this banal work of sorting this and sorting that* (socks, the refrigerator, groceries, winter clothes) *can't be that important!* But as our group discussion continued, I understood that it was more important than I'd realized.

Merton knew that obedience in the simplest tasks mattered. Obedience was inherent in following Christ. For Merton, the ordinary work was not insignificant or less important than times of prayer. Attentive obedience to the work asked of him had meaning for himself and for others.

It may seem like a stretch, but in an instant I understood that cleaning out the junk drawer had something to do with the glory of God in the world. Over the next few days, in deep decluttering mode, we filled up and carted out 14 bags to Goodwill.

Without the muddle of mess on the counter, I noticed the plant on the window ledge. When did it flower? There it was, blooming and singing with life. Beauty was there, and for a moment, anyway, I beheld it. I contemplated the beauty of that flower and I recognized the Giver.

In *Reed of God*, Caryll Houselander wrote,

> *There are many people in the world who cultivate a curious state which they call "the spiritual life." ... The only time that they do not regard as wasted is the time they can devote to pious exercise ... All the time spent in earning a living, cleaning the home, caring for the children, ... cooking, and all the other manifold duties and responsibilities, is regarded as wasted. Yet it is really through ordinary human life and the things of every hour of every day that union with God comes about.*

I wouldn't have thought that reading a biography of a monk in a monastery would help a mom in her messiness, but it did. Again and again, reading literature connects me to meaning in my days and helps me to see in new ways.

A BOOK SHOWED ME A WHOLE NEW WAY TO UNDERSTAND HOUSEWORK

"I joined WRM mainly because I was asked to, and because I liked Serena and Marcia, who proposed it to me. I didn't get to spend much time with them, and I wanted to know them better. But I also joined WRM in search of something—I didn't know what it was, but it was something along the lines of "trying to take my own life more seriously."

"I didn't think my own terrible cleaning habits would come into the equation at all. I mean, who cares, right? Cleanliness is next to godliness and all that

---

73

jazz—sounds like something a type A person would say. And I'm not type A—I'm a free spirit, gosh darn it. Why pick up toys when they're just going to get dumped back out anyway? There are so many other, more important things to do.

"Imagine my surprise when Willa Cather, one of my favorite authors, described Quebec in exactly the terms I remembered from my time there. Imagine me, a sojourner here, in Texas of all places, transported back to Quebec, where I met my husband and some of my closest friends. Imagine my chagrin over Cecil's conversation with her mother, in which her mother explains how she has come to treasure her household duties, and how Cecil will, too. "Yeah right," I thought.

"Shadows on the Rock is a very beautiful novel, but my favorite part of the book is when Cecil returns from a visit to a family in the wilderness. When Cecil is back in her own kitchen, holding her own tools, she realizes that "these were the tools with which she made reality." It's in that moment that all of the housework she has done for her father and in honor of her mother actually becomes her own.

"Those words struck me. "These are the tools with which she made reality." Finally, a reason to clean up! Not just a reason to clean up, but an explanation of the beauty of work, any work, even mopping floors and washing dishes. Work, our work, my work, is an extension of creation. We take part in the creation of reality. We aren't just putting things back where they started—we are building an environment in the present.

"It would be folly to say that I now enjoy cleaning up, but it would be fair to say that now I can face the tasks in front of me with a certain joy, knowing that the care of the home is the creation of reality—a reality that is beautiful, an extension of the love of the Father, and even a strike back against the forces of chaos."

—Claire Vaidyanathan

"The world will never starve for want of wonders, but for want of wonder."

—G. K. Chesterton

"When she was half a dozen years younger, Louisa had been overheard to begin a conversation with her brother one day by saying, 'Tom, I wonder' — upon which Mr. Gradgrind, who was the person overhearing, stepped forth into the light and said, 'Louisa, never wonder!'"

—Charles Dickens, *Hard Times*

"As soon as all the people saw Jesus, they were overwhelmed with wonder."

—Mark 9:15a (NIV)

"Words are windows into mystery."

—Malcolm Guite, "De Magistro"

"I would sooner live in a cottage and wonder at everything than live in a castle and wonder at nothing."

—Joan Winmill Brown

Chapter 5

Books Open a Window to Wonder

Sometimes when I look up at the night sky, I experience the wonder of creation, of things hidden and things revealed. Questions spring forth: *Why am I here? How do I fit into all of this? What is the meaning of life?* Psalm 8 comes to mind: "What is mankind that you are mindful of them, human beings that you care for them?"

WONDER AS A WAY OF SEEING

Wonder looks for—and sees—meaning, beauty, possibilities, hope. Animals don't imagine. They don't have the capacity. Your dog doesn't sit around and wonder about how he can make a difference in the world or cook a beautiful meal. But human beings *do* think about these things because we have this imaginative faculty, the ability to wonder.

It's a unique part of being human. But there is a catch. The capacity to wonder can be stifled, either intentionally or inadvertently. Perhaps it gets stifled because we don't value it, or the people around us don't value it.

Wonder must be continuously cultivated if we want it to thrive. Why do we want it to thrive? For one, it helps us grow in understanding and empathy. In a world that seems to be increasingly bent on seeing people as a means to greater efficiency or as pawns in a power game, wonder sees people in another way—as individuals created in the image of God.

Another reason is that wonder helps us realize the glory of creation. Have you ever stepped outside on a crisp autumn day and been struck by the overwhelming beauty of the trees, the air, and the sunlight? Wonder opens our eyes to the splendor in front of us.

Yet another reason to develop the mindset of wonder is that it strengthens our capacity to imagine. We need imagination in order to hope. We need imagination to empathize with other people and their experiences, which are different from our own.

Reading literature exercises our imaginations and keeps our sense of wonder alive. Great novelists invite us to picture deeper realities and the interconnectedness of things. As we read, we begin to recognize these beautiful realities in our own lives, too.

WONDER MAKES US MORE HUMAN—AND MORE FUN!

I read *Hard Times*, by Charles Dickens for WRM's Year of the Contemplative. Dickens strikes a hard blow against utilitarianism. While we no longer live in the 1800s, our technological age is rife with utilitarianism. Technology—combined with our frantic efforts to get ever more done—demands ever greater efficiency. And with greater efficiency comes a grave temptation to view human beings in a reduced, dehumanized way. We're judged by how much we accomplish.

He seems to suggest an antidote to the hard times brought about by the mechanization of the Industrial Age. Not surprisingly, this solution comes through women! The characters who have cultivated wonder are the ones who are able to bring a healing, humanizing gaze on those they meet.

In Mr. Gradgrind's "Facts, nothing but facts" school of efficiency, his students are "never to fancy and never to wonder." Their education stifles their growth.

Dickens shows us that women who live with wonder have a unique ability to impact their surroundings; they are the ones who create an environment in which people can thrive. The character Sissy Jupe, for example, illustrates that true femininity is a remedy for the utilitarian mindset. It is part of the solution to restore social harmony. The people Sissy interacts with realize they are loved; love brings out the best in them.

Mrs. Gradgrind, on the other hand, buys into her husband's utilitarian system. Her feminine nature becomes cold and complaining—to the extent that she is unable to enjoy being with her children. When she walks into the room and sees her children wasting time in a state of wonder as they sit gazing into the fire, she resents it and lets them know it: "I really do wish that I had never had a family, and then you would have known what it was to do without me!" Rather than joining her children to wonder and delight in the fire, she nags and complains. Her eyes and heart are shut tight.

Mrs. Gradgrind's closed heart shocked me because in it, I saw myself. How many times do I complain and nag? How often do I look at my husband and children through a lens of efficiency instead of a lens of delight?

Years ago my son Jim came home from an event and said, "Mom a lady who was there knew you, and she said it must be so much fun having you as a mom." By the look on his face, I could see he was surprised by her thinking I must be fun. I said, "You don't think I'm fun?"

"Well, you're a good mom and everything, but I wouldn't say you're fun."

This little conversation with Jim was a wakeup call for me. I took a look in the mirror and saw a mean, stern-looking mom whose primary concern was to keep a houseful of kids under some kind of control. But that little exchange made me wonder: *How can I live with my children differently? Is it possible to enjoy them in the midst of all the work involved in managing a household?* I prayed. I asked. I begged the Lord to help me.

Later that day, an idea came to me that was a step toward living with wonder. I got a pad of yellow post-it notes and put messages to myself around the house where I would see them. My mantras became, "Laugh every day with each child"; "Look each child in the eye everyday"; "Delight in each child every day."

These little post-it notes stirred up my curiosity and creativity—sending me on a quest: *What is there today to delight in and laugh with*

Margaret about? I wondered. As I walked into the kitchen, there was six-year-old Margaret to let me know: "Look, Mom, I did my nails!" she said with pride as she stood there with the jar of olives open and a green olive secured on each of her 10 fingers. Before my resolution, I might have reacted in anger; that day, a little miracle happened in me. I found myself smiling and then laughing. I saw Margaret through the eyes of  wonder: Who is this creative happy, beautiful child? *Thank you, God, for giving me eyes to see her in a new way.*

Children are good at reminding us to see. Antoine de Saint Exupéry's Little Prince teaches the narrator, "It is only with the heart that one sees rightly. What is essential is invisible to the eyes."

Good literature can awaken us to see and to live a more *wonderful* life, that is, a life more full of wonder.

When I Read, I See More

Reading keeps me living in a state of openness to my own journey. I somehow seem to see myself in every book.

Victor Hugo's *Les Misérables* stretched my capacity to see.

My imagination filled with a glimpse of goodness as I read about the daily duties of the saintly Bishop Myriel. Over the course of the book, I watched Jean Valjean grow in charity, in forgiveness, in fortitude. My own desire to live like this exploded. Performing hidden works of mercy, doing good for others—I could see this is the most attractive way to live.

The setbacks Valjean faces parallel setbacks in my own life. Valjean must return to prison. I, too, find myself time and again back in my own prison—old ways of thinking that keep my heart hardened and locked away from others. Will these setbacks and personal failures extinguish my hope? Or can I, like Valjean, see them as part of my journey? I want to grow and change the way this humble hero does.

Again and again, Valjean moves from chaos to order. At one point in the novel, he has escaped from prison and is on the run. Officer Javier is again at his heels. With young Cosette on Valjean's back, chaos ensues. Just when it seems there is no way to escape from the situation that is closing in on him, he scales a seemingly insurmountable wall and jumps down on the other side of it, finding himself right in the middle of a convent garden. Just like that, Valjean moves from the height of chaotic suspense to serene order. He escapes the prison of criminals to land within a freely chosen "prison" of nuns.

Life is this way. We move from chaos to order and from order to chaos.

As I was reading this novel, my mom suffered a stroke. Our family had to navigate through this upheaval and change of events. But over the weeks, a new normal was established, and the time of chaos moved to one of order.

Seeing my life against the backdrop of the novel, I saw myself in the midst of the ebb and flow of life with the hand of God guiding all the circumstances. Questions surfaced. *Why is trauma a part of life? Why do I resist taking risks in certain situations? What risks are wise to take? Am I aware that I, too, am a protagonist in history?*

Jean Valjean lives to do good. The novel is the story of his ongoing conversion. His life makes a difference in the lives of others. He makes choices and takes risks that result in a more beautiful way to live.

When I read a great book such as *Les Misérables*, I not only enter a time in history, I enter a relationship with the characters. A story provides a rare glimpse of what an intentional life looks like and how people can change over time. We have a chance to see a life lived through the lens of time. In chapter one, Valjean is identified only by his prison number, 24601 By the end of the story, I feel I know him as a friend.

LIFELONG LEARNING

It's never too late to learn how to learn. We all have different experiences and opportunities.

There was a young man who went off to college in the early 1970s. Like many of us, he was aware that he hadn't received the best high school education, but "Providence stepped in," he said,

> I went to the University of Kansas, and I learned about a program that was being offered there called the Integrated Humanities Program. There was no religious motivation at all for me to get involved in the program; it just sounded interesting. The program was started by two English professors and one classics professor. They were very good teachers. They had discovered that students really had not been exposed to the great things of Western culture—literature, poetry, music—things that were part of the staple of education a generation or two before.

The professors wanted to introduce their students to these beautiful things that had been taught through the ages. In this program, they read the classics and, he went on to say, "students fell in love with this beautiful literature, we fell in love with learning, and we became excited about learning because of these beautiful things. Beauty attracted us to these great ideas—like truth, goodness, and beauty—as they are lived out in books, but also as we . . . lived them out in our lives."

The young man who was introduced to the humanities is now a bishop—Bishop James Conley from Lincoln, Nebraska.

My experience was different. I attended a state college and received a practical education. For the most part, I learned facts. I jumped through hoops. I gained knowledge. But the humanities, the arts, philosophy, and literature were minimal or lacking completely. Even though I earned several degrees and attained employment, deep down, something was missing in my education.

This is how I believe it has been for many of us who were educated in the last twenty to forty years. We have a sense that we missed out on something in our education but we have no idea what that might be. Anne Delaney, the protagonist in Michael O'Brien's novel *Strangers and Sojourners*, says of her students, "They were hungry but they did not know they were hungry." That describes many of us.

Now that we're adults, we're on our own to continue our education. How do we do this? What satisfies the hunger for that "something" more? Worthy books that have stood the test of time have become, for me, an ongoing source of education where my hunger is awakened and fed. These great books are the best "school" I've found. They help me learn to really see my own life and the world around me.

When I was reading *Kristin Lavransdatter*, I learned something about myself that helped me be a better wife. There is a point in this novel where Kristin's husband, Erlend, who has been gone a long time finally returns to their estate, but Kristin has been hurt so many times that she will not open her heart and let her husband back into family life. She shuts him out. As I read, I found myself siding with Erlend and begging, *Kristin you've got to let him in. He's trying, and your heart is so hard. Let him into the life of the family.* And then suddenly I recognized myself in the story. I realized that often when my husband Pete would come home from work, I would tend to shut him out. Reading the story of Kristin allowed me to see that Pete needed to be invited back into family life when he came home. It was an easy thing I could do. Through this medieval classic I saw something in myself, and this insight changed the way I responded to my husband.

Several weeks after this "aha" moment, Pete came into the kitchen where I was chopping carrots for dinner. What he said surprised me: "Marcie, I don't know if I'm imagining this or what, but you sure have

been nicer to me lately." I had to chuckle and say to myself, *Thank you, Kristin!*

When our group met to discuss this book, I discovered I wasn't the only one touched by this fourteenth-century Norwegian woman. She had us shedding tears of laughter and tears of pain. By seeing a horizon different from our own, we were helped in a non-threatening way to see our own lives. That's the surprise of it!

DISCOVERING MY HEART

"I'm so grateful to read these good books with other women. I'm coming to understand how these authors are my friends because they know my heart in a way that I don't know it—but in a way that I'm discovering it. I notice that when I'm not engaged in one of these great works, I'm not as aware of the greatness of my life, and the greatness of my desire, and the drama of everything that's present in the little everyday things with kids and with my husband. In my reading group, we're talking about the most real things that are brought to us in these great works."

—Stephanie Stokman

THE WONDER OF GREAT BOOKS

It is not by accident that classic books have stood the test of time. Generations of readers have found them to be lights to live by.

But the world is changing. As we become more accustomed to digital reading and quick, surface-level reading, we come dangerously close to letting these books fall from our "To Be Read" lists. After all, many of them are long, and the writing style may be outdated and difficult to work through.

I find that my commitment to help other women read well keeps me returning to the classics—and I'm continually grateful for the wisdom I find there.

My daughter Beth is one of the women who helps me remember the value of great books. A couple years ago, I almost decided to pull Victor Hugo's *Les Misérable* off the reading list for WRM's Year of the Pilgrim. I thought it was just too much to ask of the women to read this hefty novel since we had read *The Divine Comedy* just the year before. When Beth saw this book was missing from the list, she called me right away. "Mom where is *Les Mis*? I don't see it as one of next year's books?"

"Beth, I thought this book would just be too much for us to read, so I replaced it with a shorter novel."

"Mom!" I could hear she was serious about this. "Mom, you've got to put *Les Mis* back on the list! My group is looking forward to it. Mom, when will we read a novel like this if we don't read it together? That's why we stay together, to help each other read great books that we won't read on our own. Don't lower the bar!"

See the kind of pressure I am up against? I was torn.

There is a fine line when it comes to raising the bar. It can become an insurmountable obstacle. Some of the women in Well-Read Mom groups are new to this type of reading. Others are just not able to finish a book of this length in the midst of an unusually demanding season. But because of my daughter's cry, *Les Mis* was added back on the list, and I am glad it was. Yes, it was long. No, it wasn't easy. But yes, it was worth it. Once again it opened my heart to greatness.

Great books—by the way they are written and by the stories they tell—ask to be read deeply. When we read online, it is often to seek information. But deep reading is a different kind of reading. It is relational. A dialogue happens between the author and the reader. I know when I am reading deeply because I relax and experience a sense of active, engaged enjoyment. It is like Lucy entering the wardrobe into the realm of C.S. Lewis's Narnia—the book is a whole other world.

READING EXPANDS OUR HORIZONS

Regular reading takes us to a place where we are able to view situations and circumstances from a variety of angles.

According to Professor Mary Reichardt, "Any of the liberal arts expands us from our own narrow worlds and egos—they are 'liberating,' and that's where the word *liberal* comes from in this context. Literature, in particular, allows us to enter the lives of others, past, present, and future."

Near the end of his book *An Experiment in Criticism*, C. S. Lewis writes, "This, so far as I can see, is the specific value of good of literature; . . . it admits us to experiences other than our own."

Reading takes us into the life of others, allowing us to see the world at a different time, in a different place, or from a different perspective, and in this way it, surprisingly, gives us a clearer vision of our own lives.

"We are now suffering collectively from a 'tyranny of the virtual,' since we find ourselves unable to look away from the screens that mediate not just print but, increasingly, reality itself."

—Will Self, "The Printed Word in Peril,"
Harpers Magazine, October 2018

"If you do not learn to read, that is, read with pleasure, that is, make the breakthrough into the delight of reading—you are going to miss out. . . . I mean that, no matter what you go into—law, medicine, computer science, housewifing, house-husbanding, engineering, whatever—you are going to miss out, you are not going to be first-class unless you've made this breakthrough. You are going to miss out, not only on your profession, but on the great treasure of your heritage, which is nothing less than Western civilization."

—Walker Percy

Chapter 6

Deep Reading Preserves the Access Code

I was sitting on the couch with my kids just after coming home from the library. "Mom, try this Magic Eye book. Can you see the castle?" The colors and shapes were mesmerizing, but I certainly didn't see a castle.

Not everyone who looks at the two-dimensional pictures in a Magic Eye book can see the three-dimensional images within the patterns. It requires diverging one's eyes in a certain way—a technique that can be learned, apparently, through practice.

Reading novels is like this. It's possible to read the two-dimensional words on a page without entering the three-dimensional world of the book.

Today more than ever, it's easy to miss out on the whole experience of deep reading. We spend a significant amount of time reading from screens, which makes us very good at scanning and skimming. While this skill is necessary because of the constant barrage of information coming at us, we can get stuck in that mode. Scanning and skimming becomes our normal way to read.

But in good literature, there is much we can only access by reading deeply.

WHAT IS DEEP READING?

The capacity to read and the capacity to enter the zone of deep reading are two different things, just as the ability to walk and the ability to enjoy a serious hike are two different things. The more we develop a skill, the more enjoyment we can experience as we use it. The basic ability to read words and sentences is primary. But there is the potential for so much more. When we train our brains to engage in deep reading, we develop a skill that allows us to experience greater enrichment and satisfaction.

The deep reader, protected from distractions and attuned to the nuances of language, enters a state that psychologist Victor Nell, in his article "The Psychology of Reading for Pleasure: Needs and Gratifications," likens to a hypnotic trance. Nell found that the pace of reading actually slows when readers are enjoying themselves the most. The combination of fast, fluent decoding of words with slow, unhurried progress on the page gives deep readers time to enrich their reading with reflection, analysis, and their own memories and opinions. It gives them time to establish an intimate relationship with the author or the characters.

Remember that scene in *Anne of Green Gables* where Anne and Marilla are walking down the path together hand in hand? Marilla says she doesn't like to read books. Young Anne—an avid reader with a vivid imagination—says with sympathy, "Oh, Marilla, how much you miss!"

Marilla strikes us as a capable woman who can read perfectly well—certainly well enough to read the news and find out whatever she needs to know—but because she doesn't read books, there is much that she misses.

READING IN A DIGITAL CULTURE

If you, like many of us, find that it does not come naturally to deeply concentrate on a novel, don't give up.

A Pew research survey, published in the *Atlantic* in 2014, stated that the number of non-book readers has nearly tripled since 1978. Concentrating is more difficult than it used to be; people find it is less natural to sit down with a printed book. Reading online feels much more compelling.

"Between blog posts, Twitter feeds, listicles, and long-winded Facebook rants, everyone seems to be reading something most of the time—right from the palm of their hand. Yet we don't seem to be better readers. In fact, we seem to be worse," claims English professor Karen Swallow Prior in *Christianity Today* (January, 2019). She points out that digital reading teaches our brains to move quickly over a lot of material and to veer off on rabbit trails, hopping from one link to another, never holding our attention long on any one idea. We become addicted to fresh stimulation—every minute a new image or a new Tweet. Reading becomes more like indulging in a bag of M&Ms than like savoring a nourishing meal.

And since we're so full from the candy, we don't have an appetite (or the time) for books.

Besides, if no one around us is reading books and everyone is talking about (or forwarding) some recent post, the winds of culture blow us along, and here we are—on our phones again.

DOES IT MATTER HOW WE READ?

What's wrong with reading online?

While researchers still know very little about the effects of digital reading, they do know it alters the brain; digital reading is somehow reshaping our brains' circuitry so that we gradually lose our capacity to concentrate for sustained periods of deep reading.

Dana Gioia, former chairman of the National Endowment for the Arts, says, "I would believe people who tell me that the Internet develops reading if I did not see such a universal decline in reading ability and reading comprehension on virtually all tests. What we are losing in this country is the sustained, focused, linear attention developed by reading."

Technology writer Nicholas Carr, author of "Is Google Making Us Stupid?" gives the same prognosis: "What the Net seems to be doing is chipping away my capacity for concentration and contemplation."

My experience is similar. I went through a time of life where reading a novel seemed absolutely out of the question. Surviving was what

I needed to focus on. If I had time for a book, it seemed to me I needed self-help books—every self-help book out there! I missed the days of getting into a novel and the sense of satisfaction that went with it, but when I tried to pick up *Silas Marner* and read a few pages, I became concerned. I did not seem to be able to focus or concentrate or remember what I was reading. Alarmed, I rationalized, *This would be a waste of my time anyway right now. How can I justify taking time learning about life in the 1800s, when I don't know how I'm going to get a meal on the table this evening?*

In truth, I was out of practice and didn't know how to get back into reading good literature. Having trained my brain to skim for efficiency, I found myself attacking the novel the with the same get-it-done mentality I used online. But to skim through a novel in this way is to miss the deep dive where the treasure lies.

SLOW READING

"We eat too fast," my husband lamented one day as we sat down to dinner. He had just gotten home from a conference on disease prevention, where he learned that this simple lifestyle change—eating more slowly—could improve our health. One of the negative side effects of racing through a meal is that the brain's natural signal that lets us know we are getting full doesn't have time to register. Not only that, but rushing a meal doesn't allow us to connect with and enjoy one another, causing us to miss out on interactions that build family life.

There's fast food, and there's slow food. Each fills a different need. Just so, there's fast reading, and there's slow reading. Each fills a different need. We need to be bi-literate, both digital and deep readers, able to maintain our skills in both kinds of reading.

Reading more and reading well is not about speed-reading. It usually means just the opposite, reading fewer words but gleaning more meaning and enjoyment from them.

When we pick up a novel, we need to remind ourselves to *slow down*. The idea is to enter into the world of the text. If I don't intentionally switch to a slow-read mindset, I soon realize that I have not focused and have almost no idea what I have just read. It has been helpful to realize this difference and to be intentional about switching modes. In the end, it is better to read one chapter in deep-reading mode than to skim through an entire book without grasping the meaning.

What are the benefits of slow-reading? Growing in the ability to think critically is one. Other benefits include our increased ability to make connections, engage with the story in a thoughtful way, and comprehend more of the meaning of the text. These benefits are worth our while.

The built-in limits of print safeguard the gateway to deep reading. On the printed page, because we can't click in and out of the text, switch to another tab, or check our email, we must surrender to the story and follow where the author leads. This type of reading is conducive to the deep reading experience.

While there is no doubt that reading literature is work, the surprise for me is that it is pleasurable work. I can feel myself relaxing. I'm not in charge; I can just receive what is unfolding in the narrative. What I never expect is that reading a thousand-page book like *Anna Karenina* can be a stress-relieving, satisfying experience. But it is!

Enjoying both a great meal and a great book are ways of reminding ourselves that the things that matter most are timeless. They are worth preparing for and then taking time to enjoy.

TOO MUCH STIMULATION?

"We were never born to read," says Dr. Maryanne Wolf in her book *Proust and the Squid: The Story and Science and the Reading Brain*.

Her point is that reading is not something genetically programmed into us. Human beings created written languages as civilizations developed. Reading is an acquired skill that must be nurtured, protected, developed, practiced, and—of utmost importance—passed down to future generations.

Wolf goes on to say that the fact that reading is "not natural" means that it is capable of being changed with ramifications. The brain makes a new circuit for this new function that doesn't have a genetic program. And in the process, we make new connections between visual areas and language areas and cognitive areas and affective areas. It's pretty sophisticated to combine new networks of vision and new networks of language and cognition.

Children must be taught first of all to decode letters, words, and sentences. Through practice and more practice, they achieve fluency, developing circuitry in the brain that makes connections between the books and their own lives. Beyond that, they eventually need to learn to ponder the meaning of ideas and to draw inferences. This is a precious human capacity that is worth practicing ourselves and passing on, so that we don't lose this ability and so that our children develop it.

> Wolf says, "I worry we will not use our most preciously acquired deep reading processes because we're just given too much stimulation." She is particularly concerned about future generation of readers who may never develop deep reading circuits in their brains, putting them at risk for stifled intellectual and emotional development.

USE IT OR LOSE IT: PRESERVING THE CAPACITY TO READ DEEPLY

The ability to draw wisdom from great literature is a treasure. It's like having an access code to all the riches of civilization. Have you ever forgotten your password at an ATM machine? You may have thousands of dollars in your bank account, but if you don't know your access code, you can't retrieve your money. In a similar way, there is treasure in great and worthy books, but without the ability to deep read, we will be shut out from the wealth of wisdom that is ours. Deep reading is the access code that lets us retrieve and comprehend the treasure that is there for us.

Many people are finding it difficult to concentrate when they try to read from a book. This problem has a solution: start reading. The deep-reading "muscle" is like other muscles. The way to strengthen it is to use it. Reading researcher Dr. Maryanne Wolf recommends 20-30 minutes of book reading daily to develop and maintain the habit of deep reading.

Three Ways to Help Our Children Become Deep Readers

As parents, we can't assume that our children will automatically develop a capacity for deep reading. Our task is not just to maintain our own capacity to read deeply, but to safeguard the development of this ability in our children. We can do this in three ways.

One way is to model deep reading for them. When our children see us enjoying good books, they come to understand that reading good books is enjoyable.

A second way is to read aloud to our children. Start with nursery rhymes, which introduce little ears to the joy of language. Later we can read them stories and talk about those stories.

Third, once our children become fluent readers, we can continue reading aloud to them—because sharing books is one of the best bonding experiences. It encourages them to read good books for enjoyment, not only to find information. We encourage them in this discipline so they won't miss out on the delight of reading for pleasure, an experience that enlarges their ability to think and reason and grow as human beings.

I feel strongly about encouraging parents to continue (or begin again!) reading from books and to help their children do the same. What a tragedy it would be to lose the access code to so many treasures of our culture. Books can easily be preserved digitally, but will future generations have the level of reading ability to engage with these texts in such as way as to be able to glean the wisdom within them?

Detaching from Devices

"Observing young people's attachment to digital devices, some progressive educators and permissive parents talk about needing to 'meet kids where they are,' molding instruction around their onscreen habits. This is mistaken," says Maryanne Wolf. "We need, rather, to show them someplace they've never been, a place only deep reading can take them."

"Many forms of natural revelation declare the glory of God. But for me, great books have bridged the gap between truths contained in the Bible and their application to my life."

—English professor Karen Swallow Prior

"When you reread a classic, you do not see more in the book than you did before; you see more in yourself than there was before."

—Clifton Fadiman

"The reading of Dante is not merely a pleasure, a tour de force, or a lesson; it is a vigorous discipline for the heart, the intellect, the whole man."

—British statesman W. E. Gladstone

Chapter 7

Good Books Can Be a Path to Virtue

As part of the annual New York Encounter cultural event several years ago, Well-Read Mom arranged a reading of selected letters from C. S. Lewis's book *The Screwtape Letters*. This book is made up of a series of fictional advice letters from a senior demon to his young nephew, who has been assigned to tempt a human "patient." After this reading, a young man approached me. I thanked him for attending, but he said, "No—thank you. You don't understand. I needed to hear this. I see myself in the patient. I've been away from the church, and I've believed these tricks of the Devil. I need to come back to church." I later learned that he followed through on that decision. *The Screwtape Letters* helped him to see the choices he was making in his own life. The book awakened his imagination and helped him to change course.

C. S. Lewis was an atheist in his youth, but he was a reader with a superbly well-trained mind and imagination. Books were an important part of his conversion to Christianity. When he happened to pick up the book *Phantastes*, by George MacDonald, on the sale rack in a railway station, it introduced him to a vision of true goodness. It captivated him. He later said that MacDonald's novel "baptized [his] imagination." It awakened him to the reality that virtue is beautiful and desirable. This insight was a key step in his journey to faith.

Great books serve as milestones along the path to faith and maturity for many of us. Some books have had such a profound impact on people that they've altered the course of history.

Harriet Beecher Stowe's *Uncle Tom's Cabin*, for example, helped to awaken the moral imagination of the American people before the Civil War. For decades, abolitionists had tried to bring an end to the evils of slavery by quoting statistics and holding rallies. But it was Stowe's novel that made Americans fall in love with Uncle Tom, Eliza, and little

Harry. Readers agonized when Uncle Tom was torn from his family. The book helped them realize that slavery is an injustice against real human beings—with moms and dads and children just like their own. *Something must be done!* When Harriet Beecher Stowe eventually met Abraham Lincoln, he addressed her as "the little lady who started this war." He recognized the impact of her novel on changing the minds and hearts of many who read it.

"Until very recent years, men took it for granted that literature exists to form the normative consciousness—that is, to teach human beings their true nature, their dignity and their place in the scheme of things. . . . The end of great books is ethical—to teach us what it means to be genuinely human," said political theorist Russell Kirk.

Good literature helps to form our consciences by working through our imaginations. It shows us what it looks like to flourish (or not) as individuals and also to live well (or not) with our neighbors. In a novel, not only do we follow the events in a story, we are also privileged to get a glimpse into the inner thought-life of the characters as they make decisions.

WHAT MAKES "GREAT BOOKS" GREAT?

My idea of a "great book" is one in which the author shares a deep and true understanding of the human condition. When I read Tolstoy or George Eliot, I find myself saying, "Yes! That's how it is! Now I see it more clearly!"

Many of the Western classics are written from a Judeo-Christian worldview—even if the authors aren't writing a specifically "Christian" story. They show us people like ourselves, each with a unique but fallen nature. We see sin and its consequences. We see the need for redemption. Oftentimes we get to see redemption—not that all plots need a happy ending.

In the Judeo-Christian viewpoint, reality isn't an illusion or nothingness. It is *real*: a good world full of free human beings who are fallen and continue to make choices with real consequences. This beautiful but broken reality is where we live. It is the territory through which we make the journey of life.

The novel is an art form well suited to convey this pilgrimage. Time matters. Place matters. Things happen for a reason. Circumstances are not incidental, but rather relevant landmarks as the characters navigate their way home.

A PATH TO VIRTUE

"We must imagine what virtue looks like in order to act virtuously," explains Karen Swallow Prior in her 2018 book *On Reading Well*. In this book, Prior expounds on twelve great books, each illustrating (positively and/or negatively) a different virtue. She points out that reading itself—if we do it well—is "formative, not merely informative." The act of deep reading stretches our minds, strengthening our ability not only to read texts, but also to read people and situations. We can grow in wisdom.

Novels, short stories, and poetry use figures of speech, which enrich our store of images and increase the connections between different parts of our brains. As we read, we learn to see multiple layers of meaning. "Literary language," says Prior, "encourages habits of mind, ways of perceiving, processing, and thinking that cultivate virtue by reminding us of the meaning that cannot be found apart from telos." By *telos* here, she means the purpose for which God created us.

FORMING THE MORAL IMAGINATION

Human beings have a unique capacity to imagine. The imagination is what allows us to perceive more than what is immediately before our eyes. We ponder the universe. We can live with a sense of wonder. We ask questions like, "Why am I here?" and "What is the meaning of life?"

As we read, our imagination allows us to grow in empathy for people whose situations may be different from our own. But here's the catch: this imaginative capacity must be developed.

What is the moral imagination? British philosopher Edmund Burke defined it this way: "The moral imagination aspires to the apprehending of right order in the soul and right order in the commonwealth."

Our moral imagination is similar to a worldview. Where *worldview* sometimes refers only to information in the mind, *moral imagination* includes virtues that shape the way we live. It motivates our behavior and gives us wisdom to deal with life situations.

Scripture and liturgy are the primary influences that rightly order our imaginations to truth. In the Christian story, we come to see who we are. Our relationships are ordered: we are sons and daughters of the Father, and because we share our Father in common, we are brothers and sisters. We learn our story, the story of Creation; the Fall; and the life, death, and resurrection of Christ. The Christian story brings the meaning of life into focus. Our imaginative view of the world is unified. In this story, each person has infinite value.

The Christian story gives meaning to all of life, including suffering. From serious circumstances, like my mom's dementia and my friend's miscarriage, to everyday banal experiences like trying to find a lost sock and keep the house in order—in this story, everything has meaning. Our life experiences have the possibility of being lifted into this Great Story where there is a mysterious connection between the visible and invisible worlds. Rightly ordered imaginations help us to perceive that God is at work in reality.

The arts—especially literature—are another way to cultivate the moral imagination. For the mind to gain access to the imaginative world, it needs some essential material on which it can work. Stories can provide that material. I heard about a pastor and his wife who studied theology and the Bible every day. One day they heard a talk about the importance of literature, so they began to read C. S. Lewis's *Chronicles of Narnia* aloud together. At one point the wife stopped her husband in the middle of his reading: "Tom, something has been missing from our lives and it is the imagination!" This woman understood at that moment that truth was being communicated, and this was happening through her imagination.

In this secular age, we need all the help we can get to awaken our imagination in a way that helps us move toward what is beautiful, good, and true. Worthy books fill our imaginations with possibilities for facing life with faith, hope, love, gratitude, courage, fortitude, temperance, moderation, justice, and mercy.

GROWING IN EMPATHY

As we read deeply, we create mental pictures of the unfolding drama of the story. Our imagination draws on the same regions of the brain that would be active if the event were happening in real life.

Research by Professor Anne Mangen of the Norwegian Reading Centre suggests that "as our capacity for narrative engagement is compromised by new technology, we experience less 'transportation' (the term for being 'lost' in a piece of writing), and as a further consequence become less capable of experiencing empathy." The study, as reported by Will Self, looked at real-time brain scans, which showed that reading deeply about a character's experience lit up the same parts of the brain as would be lit up if I actually lived through the experience.

Reading widely introduces us to a variety of complex characters, giving us insight into their motivation and letting us share their life experiences vicariously. This increases our ability to read people and to resonate with their joys, their sorrows, and their needs. Through the words on the page, we learn intimate details of a character's feelings and thoughts.

WHAT BOOKS CAN DO

Author Anne Lamott says it well:

"For some of us, books are as important as almost anything else on earth. What a miracle it is that out of these small, flat, rigid squares of paper unfold world after world after world, worlds that sing to you, comfort and quiet or excite you. Books help us understand who we are and how we are to behave. They show us what community and friendship mean; they show us how to live and die."

ARE THERE BOOKS WE SHOULD AVOID?

If the imagination is not formed morally, another kind of imagination can take its place. Kirk called an imagination that becomes perverse a *diabolical imagination*. Sadly, this negative imaginative view of life dominates many of the books and movies in our culture. Since books can change us, it is important to use discernment in the books we read.

What would be a reason to avoid a book?

I don't want to read anything that stirs up wrong desires. For instance, some popular romances are thinly-disguised soft pornography. That's a good reason not to read them.

Other books might not have a negative influence on the reader, but may be poorly written. The time we have to read is limited. I don't want to waste time reading a poorly-written book. That's why books that have stood the test of time are a good starting point. But of course, they are not an ending point. Many books being published today are also well written and deal with timeless, universal themes.

I love inspirational and happy books, but I wouldn't avoid a book simply because it tells a tragic story. My daughter-in-law Lisa once asked, "Why should we read these books that often make us sad?" Franz Kafka expressed what might seem like a shocking idea:

> *I think we ought to read only the kind of books that wound or stab us. If the book we're reading doesn't wake us up with a blow to the head, what are we reading for? So that it will make us happy? Good Lord, we would be happy precisely if we had no books, and the kind of books that make us happy are the kind we could write ourselves... A book must be the axe for the frozen sea within us. That is my belief.*

Another reason some people avoid books is that they show characters making sinful choices. But cautionary tales educate our imaginations and allow us to learn from the experience of the characters; this helps us face our own situations with a greater awareness of potential consequences. "A writer may, like William Faulkner, write much more of what is evil than of what is good; and yet, exhibiting the depravity of human nature, he establishes in his reader's mind the awareness that there exist enduring standards from which we fall away; and that fallen human nature is an ugly sight," explains Russell Kirk.

When an author tells the truth about the ramifications of sin, without gratuitous horror or pornographic details, our imaginations are trained to see and gain an understanding of what results from the choices of Anna Karenina, for example, in contrast to the choices of her friend Kitty.

In Gustave Flaubert's novel *Madame Bovary*, the title character Emma Bovary has been shaped by reading the wrong kind of books—romances with heroic lovers in intensely dramatic relationships. She comes to mistake romantic excitement for true love. Because of her ill-informed notion, she's not able to enjoy real life with the ordinary man she marries. She craves passion and—tragically—finds it. Some people put *Madame Bovary* on their "Do Not Read" list because the heroine has illicit affairs. But Karen Swallow Prior writes beautifully about how reading this book saved her own marriage. "Madame Bovary prevented me from cheating," she says in *Booked: Literature in the Soul of Me.*

> In seeing Emma, I simply saw myself. I sought excitement. I thought love meant external excitement and unfluctuating passion. I didn't recognize my romanticism for what it was: discontentment with what is, caused by pining for what isn't. I didn't know the difference between a real person and my idealized version of a person. Madame Bovary changed my worldview.

It's a great book that can do that.

"You don't have to burn books to destroy a culture. Just get people to stop reading them."

—Author Ray Bradbury

"All of us who wish to bring forth a renewal of Christian culture in our world should begin on our knees in prayer. But we must also begin with books in our hands, being formed in the great tradition of the classical mind."

—Bishop James Conley

"The secret of change is to focus all of your energy, not on fighting the old, but on building the new."

—Dan Millman

Chapter 8

Reading has Ripple Effects

People don't read classic literature as much as they used to. Is this a problem? I think it is. These books are full of wisdom and insight. Of course new books have a lot to offer as well, but they can't replace the great old books.

What can be done?

The best solution is a slow one: read. Reading, especially reading with others, may cause surprising and good ripple effects in our communities.

THE CLASSICS ARE AN ENDANGERED SPECIES

In an article entitled, "The Necessity of the Classics," critic Louise Cowan writes,

> We have begun to see a world in which the classics have virtually disappeared. . . . For a while we may get by on the echoes of their past glory; but when they finally have become perfectly silent, what sort of world shall we inhabit? To lose the classics is to lose a long heritage of wisdom concerning human nature, something not likely to be acquired again. Yet most college curricula now remain sadly untouched by their august presence, or at best make a gesture in their direction with a few samplings for select students. Such neglect is one of the most serious threats our society faces today.

The saying is true: "Out of sight, out of mind." When an author such as Pulitzer and Nobel Prize winner Sigrid Undset falls out of sight and off almost all college reading lists, we have a problem. We don't know what has been left behind, and most of the time we don't know that we don't know. Quietly, one by one, the great books can drop off lists and be lost from our sight. We can lose what is beautiful and true and restorative for our age.

In answer to the question, Why should we read old books? C. S. Lewis explains: "Every age has its own outlook. It is especially good at seeing certain truths and especially liable to make certain mistakes. We all, therefore, need the books that will correct the mistakes of our own period. And that means the old books."

Old books give us perspective and insight. "Those who cannot remember the past are condemned to repeat it," George Santayana famously said.

THE FIRST STEP

We cannot let ourselves be fooled into thinking that these great works are being preserved for us and for the future just because they are easily accessible online. This is not how great books become or remain integrated in our tradition. The only way to preserve what has been given to us through great literature is to partake of it ourselves.

This is the first step. It is a starting point for us to begin a renewal of culture together. It may seem like a small step, but small steps matter. We can't give what we don't have. Book by book, our imaginations are formed in ways that help us effectively interact with our families and our communities.

"Democracy requires engaged and informed citizens," says Dana Gioia, former chairman of the National Endowment for the Arts, "and the best way I know of creating and sustaining those citizens is through reading. Reading is not escapism, it is an invitation to activism. If we are serious about the future of a free society, we need to be serious about reading." Isn't this what we want? Citizens who are alive enough to see and participate in transforming their communities for the better!

READING MAKES US BETTER CITIZENS

After looking at the research on reading, former chairman of the National Endowment for the Arts Dana Gioia came to this conclusion:

"We tend to think of reading as a passive activity. You know, you sit down in a chair, you read a book. It almost seems like a way of escaping from the pressures of our daily life. What we learned was something radically different. Reading is an active, engaged enterprise that requires the use of focus, linear attention, the development of your imagination, and the use of your memory. Over time this develops a depth of interior life in the individual. It gives [readers] a heightened sense of their own destiny, of their own individuality, and then—and this is the most surprising part—because you understand yourself better, you begin to recognize that other people have lives as rich and complex as your own. This fundamentally changes the way we look at ourselves . . . and how we live in society. What this led us to was the conclusion that reading is a basic civic activity, that a healthy democracy, which requires the engaged and informed participation of individuals, is also a political system which requires readers, people who take their own lives more seriously and take the lives of the communities in which they live more seriously."

—from the video "On the Importance
of Reading and Literacy"
DanaGioia.com

LEADERS WHO WERE READERS

When ordinary people commit to the regular reading of great books, they can be spurred on and inspired to live lives of greatness.

Dorothy Day returned to the novels of Dickens, Tolstoy, and Dostoevsky again and again. Reading these authors helped Day say *yes* to her life's work with the poor. Day was a woman of deep Christian faith. Daily Mass and prayer nourished her, but so did her reading. It helped her mature and grow in her understanding that her life was to be given for something great. Rereading great books helped her continually grow in her capacity for greatness.

Pope John Paul II was similar. He recalled being "completely consumed by a passion for literature" in his youth.

Martin Luther King Jr. read Ghandi. Ghandi read Tolstoy and was so impressed by his book *The Gospel in Brief* that he wrote in his autobiography that it opened his vision to the "infinite possibilities of universal love."

All these leaders were exceptional in their understanding of the human condition. Their actions changed the world. Reading awakened their humanity and spurred them toward cultural engagement, and it can do the same for us.

Which books have given you clues to your calling? Which characters show you what it means to live with courage and faith? These are books to return to regularly.

I once met a man who told me that for a season of his life he reread *The Hammer of God*, by Bo Giertz, annually. I heard of a woman who reads *Till We Have Faces* by C. S. Lewis every year. A friend of mine taught a literature class for which *The Brothers Karamazov* was on the syllabus. Despite the novel's size, she reread the whole thing each year because she found it so life-giving. Are there certain books on your shelf that are asking to be read again? Perhaps these books are instruments God is using to shape your life and direct your engagement with the culture.

LET'S EACH DO OUR PART

Each woman has a specific job that only she can do. There is a parable that goes like this:

> There was an important job to be done and Everybody was sure that Somebody would do it.
> Anybody could have done it, but Nobody did it.
> Somebody got angry about that because it was Everybody's job.
> Everybody thought that Anybody could do it, but Nobody realized that Everybody wouldn't do it.
> It ended up that Everybody blamed Somebody when Nobody did what Anybody could have done.

Not everybody can do your job. As a woman, you have a specific work to do that nobody else in your family or in your community can do. But that doesn't mean you have to do it alone. In fact, by living in a more communal way, you are empowered to do the work that only you can do.

READING TOGETHER BUILDS COMMUNITY

When we all read the same book during the same month, there is a cultural benefit, a foundation; a common base is established from which dialogue—and therefore culture—can be built.

Several years ago, I was at an airport waiting for my flight when I noticed a woman reading *Hannah Coulter*. Since this was the Well-Read Mom selection for the month, I was curious and edged over to the woman to say, "I am reading that book, too."

A conversation began with this woman from Tennessee. She let me know she was reading it for her book club. Now I was really curious. "Does your book club have a name?"

"Yes, it's Well-Read Mom. Have you ever heard of it?" I had to laugh. *Have I heard of it? It's taking over my life!* I wanted to tell her.

Minutes later we were engaged in an in-depth conversation about Wendell Berry's idea of place. How amazing that the two of us, strangers until a few minutes before, were able to share these big ideas! There was an understanding between us because we were reading the same book.

Ripple Effect

When women read more, everyone reads more: husbands, teens, children, friends. This ripple effect sets the stage for an environment where reading is part of our communal life. In this subculture, it is normal to share books and talk about what we are reading.

Madeline, my teenage daughter's friend, told me she was reading *The Long Loneliness*, by Dorothy Day. Of course, I was excited about this and surprised. "How did you come across this book?" I asked. Tim, her youth group leader, gave it to her. Tim's wife read the book in Well-Read Mom. Then he read it. So, the book went from one woman to her husband to a student. This is an example of the ripple effect taking place.

A high school senior Nikita knocked on my door, "Would it be possible to borrow *All the Light We Cannot See* from you? Annie sent me over. A group of us are going to read it for fun." Annie's mom read the book, and now her daughter wanted to do the same with her friends.

After reading "A Christmas Memory," I overheard Lisa from my group asking a few other moms if they wanted to get together and read the short story with their daughters.

One day a few years ago, I woke up to find St. Augustine's *Confessions* open on my kitchen counter. *Who is reading this?* I wondered. My son John, home from college, later let me know: "Hey, Mom, I was hungry and got some cereal in the middle of the night. I saw this on the shelf. St. Augustine is really interesting. Have you read this, Mom? It's really good!"

My oldest son, Jim, is a surgical resident in the busiest years of his training. Yet he regularly asks, "What book is Well-Read Mom reading next?" The first time this happened, I was taken aback. "How can you be following along with our reading?" I asked. It turns out he rides his bike to the hospital at five in the morning and has kept up by listening to almost all of our selections as audiobooks. Jim and his wife Steph have shared with me how their reading (or listening to) the same books at the same time gives them something to talk about that is life-giving and refreshingly different from talking about their kids or the practical details of managing a home.

Once when John and Margaret were home for spring break, I walked into my living room to ask if either of them wanted to go for a walk with me. There sat Margaret in one chair reading Dante's *Divine Comedy* and John in another reading *The Grapes of Wrath*. I had to laugh. This seemed too good to be true (in truth, it was a rare scene). But as the kids come home from college, I notice that they see home as a place of restoration. They understand that picking a good book off our shelves is an enjoyable part of that replenishing process. They associate reading with pleasure and being home. This lays a foundation for young adults to become lifetime readers, not just school-time readers.

Every penny I've spent to build a library in my home has been worth it, if only for these moments. If the books were just on my e-reader, I doubt this would have happened. But they were on the shelf, within reach, and because of this, John encountered Steinbeck and Margaret, Dante.

Even though these little ripples may seem insignificant, they are, in fact, worth celebrating. When our families and local communities share literature, it impacts the quality of life right where we live. Multiply this possibility by similar incidents happening in thousands of homes across the country, and we see the hope of preserving something precious to us and building a richer, better future.

What is good, true, and beautiful is not preserved by locking the treasures up for safety in university library stacks or storing them digitally online. Instead, our heritage is preserved when we take part in it.

Faithfulness to tradition, composer Gustav Mahler said, "is not to worship the ashes but to pass on the flame."

Fifteen hundred years ago, Rome was sacked by barbarians, and Roman culture collapsed. Benedictine monks copied ancient texts, literally saving much of what was good and important from Roman civilization. In our time, we don't need to copy great works to preserve them; the texts themselves have never been more widespread or easily accessible. What we need today is to help one another actually *read* the books. Could it be that women who read and pass this treasure on to their families and friends are the modern-day monks preserving leaven in society?

And is it possible that our reading books together in small groups across the country will result in cultural renewal? I take courage from the English proverb, "Great ends come from small beginnings." The effect on the culture remains to be seen, but I echo my daughter-in-law's comment: "I live better when I'm in the pages of one of these books." We want to live well and live the truth of our lives. This desire is at the core of individual change. It is also at the core of social change. The choices we make matter.

When women accompany women to read the great books from our tradition, we participate in something that will help us not only to grow as women, but also to start a ripple effect that impacts our children, our children's children and our communities.

PART THREE
PUTTING IT ALL TOGETHER

"Start wherever you are and start small."

—Rita Baily

"Low-key change helps the human mind circumnavigate the fear that blocks success and creativity."

—Robert Maurer

Chapter 9

Tips for Finding Time to Read

The number one reason women give for not reading is lack of time. We know the value of reading, and we believe in it. But we are busy women, doing things that matter—being faithful to our callings.

It's true that in some seasons, life demands every single bit of our time and attention in order for us to survive or manage a crisis. But we don't want to become addicted to the adrenalin of life-in-hyperdrive. Nor do we want to despair that life will ever allow us time to invest in our own growth.

With a little creativity, most of us, during most seasons of life, can find a bit of time to read. Let's look at some possible strategies for making reading time a reality.

CULTIVATE AN ENTERPRISING SPIRIT

Mother Teresa witnessed her own biological mother dealing with a huge challenge. Her husband died and left her with minimal resources to raise her children. Faced with this dilemma, she started selling cloth. The young future saint learned from this to "greet poverty and adversity with an enterprising spirit," writes Charlotte Gray in the series *People Who Have Helped the World*.

Poverty and adversity are often financial issues, but can also affect our resources of time. When there are more demands on me than I have time to fill, I'm facing poverty of minutes. From Mother Teresa's mom we can take our cue. We can face the dilemma with an enterprising spirit, asking God for help and then using all the creativity He gives us to arrange our precious minutes in the best possible order.

REMEMBER THAT READING FEEDS YOUR SOUL

We have to keep reminding ourselves that we have a legitimate need to read. The order Mother Teresa founded, The Missionary Sisters of Charity, serves the poorest of the poor. In addition to the hours they spend in service, the sisters pray four hours a day. Additionally, study, recreation, reading, and rest are scheduled in. Because their work is so intense, they are aware of their need for continual grace. They don't miss their prayer, and they don't miss their reading time. If reading is profitable for the Missionary Sisters of Charity, reading is profitable for us!

BELIEVE DAILY LIFE CAN BE BEAUTIFUL

A little optimism opens the door to possibilities. Instead of jumping to the conclusion that I can't fit reading in, I can tap into creativity by asking myself, *What would it take for me to add a bit of deep reading into my life?* The answer will be different for every woman, but this chapter will share some practical tips that have helped others. They may spark an idea that you can apply to your life. Making time for reading will no doubt require creativity, but that's one of the gifts God has given us. He wants us to use it.

Creativity follows commitment. First we must embrace the fact that regular reading is an important part of our personal growth as lifelong learners. And it's not something to be pushed off to a later (presumably less busy) season of life. We need to make a commitment to start now. Once we make that commitment, we tend to get creative about ways to meet it. Too big of a commitment can set us up for failure, so let's start with baby steps.

TIP #1: KEEP THE GOAL SMALL

We're not talking about dropping everything else in your life so you can live with your nose in a book day and night. No. You've got a life, after all, and reading is supposed to enhance, not complicate it.

Start with reasonable goal, like 15-20 minutes a day (or around two hours a week). If this is new for you, you might even start smaller and work your way up.

Back when our fourth child was four months old, I was still 20 pounds overweight. Postpartum blues set in. Realizing I had to take action, I made a firm decision to start jogging for 30 minutes, four times a week. But this was a pretty big goal for me. I did not want to fail, so I decided to start slow and run for two minutes and then walk the remaining 28, gradually building up until I could run 30 minutes a day. From my back door, I set my watch and took off. Huffing and puffing, I had to stop, *surely that was almost two minutes?* Looking at my watch, there it was, just 35 seconds. That's all I could do that day. But I didn't give up. The next day I set the goal the goal for 45 seconds. Over time, I developed the stamina to run for two whole minutes, then 10, then 20. Eventually I was able to jog for the full 30 minutes.

Persistence and consistency in small steps pay off. Sometimes we fall into an "all or nothing" mentality. If we can't run a marathon, we don't run around the block. What I've learned is that small steps matter. Never underestimate the value of a single step.

With reading, I've seen this happen with women again and again. One woman was only able to read one chapter of St. Augustine's *Confessions* before our gathering. She had just had her sixth child, so she was doing well to read at all! Enriched by our discussion, she went home after book club and read two more chapters.

Another woman joined a WRM group but wasn't able to finish an entire book until near the end of her second year. It was her small, partial-but-faithful attempts that gradually paved the way for that accomplishment.

In his helpful little book *One Small Step Can Change Your Life*, Robert Maurer says,

> Once you've experienced the joy of taking the first step, you can decide whether it's appropriate to take another. You'll know you're ready when your current step becomes automatic, effortless, and even pleasurable. But don't let anyone pressure you.... If you ever feel yourself dreading the activity or making excuses for not performing it, it's time to cut back on the size of the step.

If 20 minutes of reading is just too much today, try five. Or if reading five days a week doesn't work, start with one day a week. There's only one rule in WRM: If you don't get the reading done, don't apologize. But do be actively engaged. Take a step and persistently persevere. Remember that you are doing something restorative for your heart.

TIP #2: MAKE A LIST OF YOUR PRIORITIES

I'm not talking about escaping from family duties. Some of our responsibilities are undoubtedly more important than reading. Of course these should not be sacrificed for the sake of reading. But we need balance and well-ordered priorities.

Here's a practical strategy for finding space in your life for reading without throwing more important priorities off balance. Try making two lists for yourself: first list the things in your life that are truly more important than reading. Then make a second list of things that are less important than reading (on most days).

This list can make it easy to know when it's okay to take a reading break. As soon as everything on your first list has been taken care of, grab your book and sit down to enjoy it for 20 minutes. Everything on the second list will still be there waiting for you when you're through.

Here's an example of what a priority list might look.

More Important Than Reading Today	Less Important Than a 20-min. Reading Break Today
Keeping my job	Being a workaholic
Getting enough sleep to be healthy and function well	Scrolling on Instagram, watching Netflix
Prayer, Bible study, regular exercise	Online shopping
Meeting my family's legitimate needs (changing diapers, kissing an owie, looking for lost car keys)	Micromanaging the details of my family's life which they are perfectly capable of handling without me (and would probably prefer to do without my interference)
Keeping promises	Agreeing to things other people want me to do, even if they don't really need my help and I don't want to participate
Eating well and feeding my family	Spending hours preparing elaborate meals that aren't necessarily blessing anyone
Putting the house back into functional order	Doing non-urgent laundry or cleaning, sorting, and decluttering
Attending my kids' and husband's most meaningful activities to show I support and love them	Attending every single activity or participating in absolutely every opportunity, even when it doesn't mean much to my kids or husband

If you haven't yet taken time to read today and you find yourself doing something on the list of "Less Important" tasks, stop. Just stop what you are doing—stop everything and set your timer for 20 minutes. Just read and don't apologize. You will be modeling something good for your children and receiving something useful for your soul. If you wait until you are cleaned up and caught up, you most likely won't read. Life is just that way.

Taking a fresh look at our priorities can help us exercise leadership over our own lives and carve out some time daily—or at least weekly—for our own formation.

TIP #3: SCHEDULE IN YOUR LEGITIMATE NEEDS, STARTING WITH SLEEP

If you have made a list of priorities in your life that are more important than reading, you know that those priorities make a huge difference in your quality of life. It requires initiative to be sure legitimate needs are taken care of, starting with sleep.

Schedule your bedtime. Leave work undone and get to bed or take a nap when you can. I once heard someone offer this advice to young moms: "In a multiple choice situation where one of the options is sleep, choose sleep."

In his book *Margin*, medical doctor Richard Swenson says, "We do not rest because our work is done, we rest because God commanded it and created us to have need of it."

There is a domino effect that happens when we get the sleep we need; everything else gets easier. It is easier to exercise. When you exercise, you have more energy. When you have more energy, you can attack the tasks at home. When your home is in order, you feel better. You can sit down and read.

When you take your legitimate needs seriously, you—by necessity—slow down. You have more power to say *no* to extraneous distractions. You breathe.

My daughter Beth takes a nap almost every day. She is often up throughout the night with a child who has a sleep disorder. Her need for sleep is paramount. She also finds time to read almost every day. Reading helps her embrace family life, so she takes this need seriously and is faithful to read as well as to nap. When I was watching her children one day, little Catherine let me know how nap time works in their family: "We can't come out of our room until Mom comes in to get us unless it's an emergency."

"What would an emergency be?" I asked, wanting to follow the routine.

"You know, like if a bear is getting us, then we can come out!"

So far there have been no bears on my watch, and the kids are growing in their understanding of regular quiet time. Many families schedule quiet time right after lunch each day. Latin American culture has made siesta time a culturally protected routine, similar to Britain's afternoon tea—another habit we would all do well to incorporate into our schedules.

What would your ideal week look like? Consider making a tentative template. Create a chart showing the days of the week and the hours of the day. Pencil in a schedule that would allow for all your legitimate needs and responsibilities to be met at a reasonable pace. Writing it down doesn't mean you'll be able to make it happen, but it will give you a goal to strive for. It also reduces the anxiety that comes from thinking there are countless things you "should" be doing right now.

TIP #4: JOIN A BOOK CLUB OR FIND A READING BUDDY

Most goals are easier to reach if we have friends to help us along the way. We talked about this need in Chapter Two. We can remind each other of our goals so we are not swept along by the distractions of our age.

We are women who desire to live the truth of our lives, and we believe in the power of literature to convey these deep truths. Still, the "sirens" call, and like Odysseus, we have been lured and distracted away from our best intentions. Good friends can "tie us to the mast" and keep us moving toward our goal.

The deadline of a book group meeting can be a huge help because it gives us an urgent excuse to read.

THE BEST USE OF A KITCHEN TIMER

When our group was reading Anna Karenina, one of the ladies ran into another woman from her group at the grocery store. "There is no way, I'm going to get this one read. I just have to accept it," she lamented. "I have 400 pages left and we meet in 10 days. It's okay, right? After all, there's only one rule in Well-Read Mom: 'If you don't get the book read don't apologize,' so I'm just not going to finish this one. There is just too much on my plate right now."

But that woman went away sad, and she began to think about her life and how she spent her days. She asked herself a question. Do I want to read or not? When will more time to read magically appear in my life? She understood at that moment that she did want to read this book, and now was the time. Creativity follows commitment. She got creative: "Let's see: 10 days, 400 pages, that's 40 pages a day."

That woman went into her kitchen, got her well-worn timer, set it for 20 minutes, took her book outside

---

on the porch steps and read for 20 minutes straight. She did the same thing later that day. Ten days later, one hour before her book club, she finished Anna Karenina. She came to the meeting with a huge sense of satisfaction and accomplishment. I know this is true because that woman was me.

TIP #5: CONSIDER A READING RETREAT

If it's tricky to work reading into your regular routine, you might try a reading get-a-way. I ended up having a reading retreat once despite myself, but it was exactly what I needed. Here's what happened.

I was nine months pregnant with our seventh child, and my husband agreed to stay home with the first six so I could make a silent retreat before the baby came. I was thrilled and thankful. As you can imagine, getting out the door leaving six kids behind was not easy. I remember straggling into the retreat center with nothing but a couple clean shirts and a pair of PJs in my bag.

Of course, I did manage to bring a basket full of books! Settling in with every intention to pray and read my Bible, I found myself falling asleep instead. On and off, I slept for most of the long weekend. When I was awake, I read Willa Cather's *O Pioneers!* for a few minutes only to fall back to sleep some more.

During my hour of spiritual direction, Fr. Larry Gillick, the blind priest who was guiding the retreat, asked me how the weekend was going. Feeling rather embarrassed, I let him know I felt guilty because I had spent most of the time sleeping and reading a novel. "I'm nine months pregnant with my seventh child," I explained. "I've been snapping at the kids and short with everyone—especially my husband. I'm grateful to be here, but should I really be reading a novel?"

"Are you enjoying it?" he asked me.

I said I was. Then in his gentle way, he let me know, "This is exactly what you should be doing. If you need to sleep, sleep! Read your novel and don't feel guilty."

I shared with him how the heroine in *O Pioneers!*, Alexandria, was giving me courage through the way she faced the extreme hardships of life on the prairie. If she could push the plow on the virgin prairie, surely I could maneuver the Maytag and keep the laundry going back home.

Fr. Gillick laughed and then, bowing his head, he began reciting a passage of *O Pioneers!* from memory:

> *But the great fact was the land itself, which seemed to overwhelm the little beginnings of human society that struggled in its somber wastes. It was from facing this vast hardness that the boy's mouth had become so bitter; because he felt that men were too weak to make any mark here, that the land wanted to be let alone, to preserve its own fierce strength, its peculiar, savage kind of beauty, its uninterrupted mournfulness.*

This blind priest was intentional about seeing beauty.

What Fr. Gillick helped me understand was that I did not need to apologize for reading. Great and worthy books stir my spirit, conjure up courage, bring needed restoration, put life in perspective, and help me live my everyday duties with greater stamina. It is not a waste of time but a good use of time.

If a reading retreat sounds good to you, do an online search for "retreat centers near me" and see what you can find. If you can't get away for a weekend, what about going to a coffee shop for a few hours on a Saturday?

TIP #6: START TODAY

Don't wait for an easier season of life or for a few days of vacation. We're talking about a lifestyle change, and the goal is to work reading into daily life.

You may be surprised to find out that you really have more control over your schedule than you had imagined. While it's true that some things can't be changed, others can be.

GOOD NEWS, BAD NEWS

A woman said to her friend, "I have some good news and some bad news."

"Tell me the bad news first," the friend said, bracing herself.

"The bad news is that a lot in my life is not working. We are in debt, my husband doesn't like his job, and our house is too small. I can't keep up and seem to be failing everywhere I turn. I don't have any time to think of self-care even though I know I need it. Things will get better someday but someday is not coming."

"Okay, what is the good news?"

"The good news is someday is now."

"What do you mean?"

"Someday things will get better, but today I can stop everything and get my closet in order.

"Someday we will save for my son's college education, but today I will open an account and deposit ten dollars.

"Someday I will get in shape, but today I will tie on my tennis shoes and walk around the block.

"Someday I will be well-read. Right now, I can take my book and read for 20 minutes."

"I loved everything about [my practice routine], the ritual that was always the same yet always new."

—George Leonard, *Mastery*

"Habits are the invisible architecture of daily life. We repeat about 40% of our behavior almost daily, so if we change our habits, we change our lives."

—Gretchen Rubin, *Better than Before*

Chapter 10

Developing a Restorative Reading Practice
You Can Do It!

It is easier—so much easier—and tempting to watch hours of the college basketball playoffs than it is to read *Middlemarch*. I keep expecting this temptation to go away, but it doesn't.

My daughter is no different. She informed me the other day, "Mom, I honestly don't think I would have read a single novel this year if it weren't for Well-Read Mom." I know what she is talking about. A book club provides that critical accountability-through-friendship piece that motivates us to develop our own personal reading practice.

In a moment of honesty, one of my high school students told me she didn't like the book *My Antonia* by Willa Cather. She thought it was boring. When I asked her which books she did enjoy, she said none of them interested her much. As we talked, I understood that she just wanted to get her homework done and check it off. Shawna was scanning and skimming her way through the selections. She was reading literature the same way she read on her phone, filtering fast. No wonder she didn't enjoy the book. She wasn't even really comprehending it. The root of her boredom seemed to stem from a lack of focused awareness and concentration.

"Shawna, the goal in this class is not for you just to get your work done. What I want so much is for you to enjoy reading. I want to help you develop a reading practice where this can happen." My response surprised her. "Let's focus on the way you read. Set a timer for ten minutes, and slow down your reading. Read for a short time in a focused way. See if you can comprehend a couple of pages."

"A couple pages? But if I go at that pace, I'll never keep up, and I'm already behind."

We worked out a plan where she could listen to an audiobook to supplement a set time of attentive reading from print. This was an important day for Shawna. It was the beginning of her reading practice. If she perseveres, she will come to know, not boredom, but pleasure and satisfaction in reading.

The goal of a reading practice is not to finish a list. It is to experience the wonder and other benefits of in-depth reading. When daily reading becomes its own reward, the student (or mom!) is on her way to becoming a lifetime reader.

WHAT IS A READING PRACTICE?

According to Thomas Sterner in *The Practicing Mind*, "The word practice implies the repetition of an activity with the purposeful awareness and intention of accomplishing an intended goal."

What is a reading practice? I'm defining it as a formed habit of reading in a focused way for a set time period. The immediate goal is to develop and maintain the ability to read deeply from print. The long-term goal is finding satisfaction and enjoyment in the process of reading.

AS PRACTICE IS PERFECTED, ENJOYMENT INCREASES

Hayden, a wrestler from my town, is on track to qualify for the 2020 Olympic team. Six days a week, rain or shine, he shows up to practice his workout. His dream hinges on many factors, but day in and day out, what's essential is for him to show up on the mat. I remember the first time I observed Hayden's practice at our local community center. Pedaling on the stationary bike, I had a great view. First, he pulled out a two-foot stool. He proceeded to do a one-legged vertical jump from the stool. After about 45 of these, I quit counting. What surprised me was not just each specific drill; he seemed to enjoy the workout itself. When it comes to wrestling, Hayden is on a journey to mastery.

As we develop a reading practice, we can recognize a journey to mastery as well. Author George Leonard defines *mastery* as "the mysterious process during which what is at first difficult becomes progressively easier and more pleasurable through practice."

The process of becoming a regular reader will be messy at times, and there will be challenges. When we are alert to potential discouragements, we can prevent them from becoming roadblocks.

EXPECT RESISTANCE WITH A NEW PRACTICE

We want instant gratification, but that is not how life works. When starting a new practice, expect some resistance from yourself.

When I was waiting for my grandson during his third piano lesson, he asked to be excused right in the middle of his lesson. Asking to borrow my phone, he called his dad. "Dad, when do you think I can quit piano?" He negotiated but to no avail.

Soon he was back in his lesson struggling through the C scale once again. The early stages of learning a new skill are difficult. It is a humbling experience, and we don't like it. This is normal. But with regular practice, what first seemed difficult can become not only easy but even pleasurable. Once a pianist can read music well enough to play songs for personal enjoyment or to entertain friends, a whole new world opens up.

If you are new to reading literature, you may find yourself trying to negotiate or sabotage your way out of this discipline by checking your phone or telling yourself you don't like to read these kinds of books. You might even conclude that you are just not a reader. The truth may be that it is difficult to build a reading practice, and you are meeting resistance. Recognize that resistance is normal and keep going.

Don't despise small beginnings, but do persevere. When it comes to building a new habit, perseverance almost always earns its reward. One day it will happen—you will experience a sense of satisfaction with your reading, and it will be a pleasant surprise.

Preparing for Practice

When it comes to exercise, I have a couple of tricks that help me get out the door and run around two miles four-to-five days a week. My method is to put on my running clothes and tie on my tennis shoes first thing in the morning. It may not sound like much of a trick, but it works for me.

Again and again, I find that if I'm dressed to run, it's more likely to happen. If my running clothes and shoes are on, I can smoothly incorporate running into my morning at some point. I've decided I have to run for at least six minutes to justify getting out the door. Once I'm out the door, I usually run the two-mile route. But whether its six minutes or two miles, running gives me a sense of accomplishment.

I found a similar strategy that has helped entice me to pick up a book in the afternoon. It centers on afternoon tea. One Christmas, my kids gave me a teapot and tea cozy. With this gift, a new ritual began. I would prepare in the morning by setting up a tray with a pretty napkin, the teapot, a cup, my book, and a pencil. I found this preparation paid off in two ways. First, the tray on the counter reminded me in the morning that a break was coming in the afternoon. Second, because the tray was sitting there inviting me to use it, I was more likely to take a reading break rather than keep working through the little ones' naptime. I reasoned I could spare 15 minutes for a break. Once I started reading, I would read as long as I could. And I didn't feel guilty. Over the years this teatime ritual has gone hand-in-hand with hours of restorative reading.

A reading practice is about being intentional to find a regular time to read. It is also about setting life up in such a way that daily reminders and built-in rewards are part of the process. They makes it easier to show up for practice rain or shine.

One other step helps me prepare to practice reading: I remind myself to switch to slow reading mode. I shut my phone off or leave it in another room. I intentionally slow down, focus, and pay attention to the printed work for a designated time.

CONCLUSION

Persevering in a reading practice has real results: hours of enjoyment, increased comprehension, and a treasured collection of books. Someday I'll pass the books on to my children, but because these books have become part of me, the ripple effect has already begun.

Before Well-Read Mom, I saw myself as a reader, but because I didn't have a structured plan or the motivation to keep me moving forward in this skill, I quit reading the kind of books I enjoyed the most.

Speaking to the women's groups back in the summer of 2012, I found myself wondering, *Why do I find it so tough to consistently follow through with something I used to love and sincerely still desire to do? And why can I make time for other things but not for reading, which is something I feel is more essential for my life?*

I was sad because most of the women I knew weren't reading literature on a regular basis and neither was I. One day a friend said, "You know, when I think about it, everything good in my life happens through friendship." I understood that her observation was profound. In fact, it was a key to unlock a more vibrant life. I realized I needed to take friendship seriously. I wanted the discipline of reading but on my own I didn't seem to have the willpower. With the proposal to stay together with friends, this desire became not just possible but something I have been faithful to for over eight years. Reading together with friends has made the difference.

Even though the one rule in Well-Read Mom is, "If you don't get the book read don't apologize," it is surprising how many of us end up finishing the books. The fact that we are meeting each month at a certain time and place puts enough accountability on us to keep us reading along. There is a thriving that comes with this kind of pressure.

It is easier to form a reading practice when others have an expectation for me to read the book. I work hard not to let them down. I also look forward to meeting with my friends. What I was unable to do for myself, I can do with my friends. And in the process, each of us is establishing a regular and satisfying reading practice. It's a win-win-win-win! By accompanying one another to read more and read well, we are harnessing the energy of a group of dedicated women and witnessing our own personal growth and formation.

I'll never forget that day my daughter Beth called lamenting, "Mom isn't there a place after college where women can get together and talk about the questions of life?" That day, I understood that my desire to read literature would only be met when my need was linked with the accountability of friendship.

Well-Read Mom started so simply, with my daughter's need to be with friends in a meaningful way and my saying, "Let's accompany one another to read really good books." We're still reading together—the two of us and our two-thousand-plus friends, all of us on a journey to live more beautiful lives, grow in friendship, and read more and read well together.

Appendix A

Reflections from WRM Participants

On Educating the Heart
by Susan Severson

I first sat down with Marcie in a small, outdated diner in Crosby, Minnesota, in 2013 while visiting my husband's family. I was a new mother deep in the throes of fatigue and unaddressed loneliness, and she a family friend of my in-laws. My husband grew up a few houses down from the Stokman family. Marcie and my mother-in-law, Teri, raised their children together, taught their children together. They laughed, cried, and grew together. They lived life together. They came into their faith together. Marcie's understanding of the importance of community is integral to the being of Well-Read Mom. Not just community as proximity—but community as a source of continued education of the heart.

So we sat there over our cold and forgotten tea and discussed motherhood and literature. Marcie told me of a fledgling idea born from her observed need of the young mothers in her life. I remember the shock and exhilaration I felt as Marcie began illuminating needs in my heart that I couldn't vocalize on my own. The discontent that came with "mom groups" revolving around play-doh recipes and the best diaper brands. What if a group of mothers could come together with art, with beauty at the center of it? What if we could come together and understand that we did not have to lose our own identity, even amidst this season of sacrifice? What if we came together, not to shed the responsibilities of our life, but to actually live our lives with fervor and excitement? And what if this continued education of our hearts would benefit not only us but our entire family as well?

Now, six years later, I can say that Well-Read Mom has done just that for me. The whole journey has been a surprise. I have made new friends (both real and fictional) and these friends have helped me live my daily life. The second Thursday of every month has been our day to come together and discuss our latest book—but it seems, the second Thursday of every month has seeped into the rest of the month as well. Well-Read Mom has blossomed into coffee dates, mountain biking excursions, laundry folding parties, shared teaching classes, even singing lessons. Well-Read Mom has been more than a book club for me. It has been a conduit to a deeper life and friendship with Christ. I am full of expectation for the years and the pages to come.

On Reading with Friends
by Fedi Fromm

Friends are those who are on the road of life with me, who are accompanying me in my daily toil of discovering what it means to live my life for something great. It's because of friends who do not let me settle, and who challenge me, that my heart is awakened and educated so that life has the possibility of being a great and beautiful journey. This is why I read. This is why I belong to WRM even though I am the woman who fits the profile of a "well-read mom" the least. I follow because of a friendship with people who love my destiny.

On Changing the Culture One Book at a Time
by Abbey Dupuy, from her blog Surviving Our Blessings

A few years ago, when I was a chronically sleep-deprived mother of a preschooler and toddler twins, I decided to start a chapter of Well-Read Mom in my living room.

It seems like a questionable decision brought on by too few hours of consecutive sleep (not unlike when I put the ketchup bottle in the dishwasher or when I machine-washed and dried my favorite wool sweater). According to lots of people who know me (and even those who don't know me but see me at Costco), my hands are full. I don't have time to start a book club. Maybe, just maybe, I could join a book club that someone else started—probably not, though, because I wouldn't have time to keep up with the reading.

That's why I love Well-Read Mom.

Since Marcie Stokman and her team have done so much of the work—choosing the books, preparing great materials to foster understanding and support discussion, and even sending out monthly audio introductions to play at our meetings—I really just have to make some snacks, clean the bathroom, and open the door for everyone to come in.

I'm not sure what I thought book club would be like, but this group has completely exceeded any expectations I had. We are reading things that matter—books that have shaped our culture and our faith and our civilization. The conversations we have had over these books stretch us beyond the limits of what is in front of us. They put us in touch with the past and the future, with different cultures and eras in which women have struggled as mothers, sisters, daughters, and friends. Some of their struggles look a lot like ours. Some look very different.

Some of these fictional characters have become my mental companions. I think about them as I would friends—pondering what they'd do in a situation, or remembering something wise they have said. My mental landscape is dotted with prairie sod houses and Russian tenements and hobbit holes and French Canadian villages and the people who occupy them. I'm so grateful to have found a little tribe of people who are also this way and who will talk with me about what we read together.

We don't just talk about books, of course, but we do always talk about books. Amazingly, when you discuss great books over a long period of time with interesting people, you get to know the people as well as the books. Literature's themes have always been life's themes—love, suffering, loss, grief, community. Discussing these themes in characters' lives broadens our view of them in our lives . . . and the intersection of life and literature is a great place to start or grow a friendship.

Book club is one of the high points of my month. Most of us knew each other when we began, but my Well-Read Mom buddies have become my closest friends. It takes commitment to read a great work of literature and discuss it, and we are committed to each other. Time is precious (and always feels in short supply), but I have never regretted the time spent reading and discussing a great book with these women.

Could a book club for moms change the world one reader at a time? I think that's exactly what is happening. It's not just a way to spend my limited free time. It is a way to improve my life. It makes me a better, more thoughtful person. When I'm a better, more thoughtful person, I am a better, more thoughtful mother, and my children can only benefit from that. I'm not sure that "better mothering through book clubs" is a thing yet, but if it's not, it has to be on the rise, thanks in large part to Well-Read Mom.

On Being Accompanied
by Eileen Larkin Wilkin

I didn't need WRM to help me become a reader, to validate my taking time for it, or to get me to read the classics. I've always loved reading, and was working through the classics on my own.

"On my own" was the part I regretted, but I didn't have time for a book club. So, I read alone, not trusting my interpretations, missing much. I didn't understand C. S. Lewis's *Til We Have Faces*. I read some Flannery O'Connor, but gave up.

Someday I'd join a book club.

"Someday" came when I was invited to join a group for "Year of the Friend" and realized I could make it work. Finally, I have companions in the journey through a variety of kinds of literature. I have a safe setting where I can brave voicing my thoughts. I've gained new insights and understanding that wouldn't have emerged without our discussions.

Thanks to WRM, I now have a satisfying understanding of Flannery O'Connor. I love *Til We Have Faces*. I can see that the "whiskey priest" in *The Power and the Glory* is a hero with a very human face. Without WRM, I wouldn't have appreciated *A Tree Grows in Brooklyn*.

I'm reminded of the saying, "Never judge a man until you've walked a mile in his moccasins." WRM has helped me walk a mile in the moccasins of many different people—a blind girl in WWII, a woman spurned by everyone but the widower she married, furry-footed hobbits—helping me consider each character through the lens of mercy.

I'm becoming a deeper, more careful reader.

No time for a book club? I've only missed one meeting since I joined.

Not smart enough for the classics? Thanks to the audio talks, Reading Companion, annual conference, and my group, I gain more from every book we read than I ever could on my own.

Don't need WRM? Not in the way I need air or food. But I need it nonetheless!

On Relocating and Connecting
by Diana Klee

Well-Read Mom's impact on my life has been substantial and far reaching. I have had a lot of change in my life the last several years. Most of my mothering years have been spent taking care of medically fragile kids and homeschooling. As a nurse who stays at home full-time, I can be a very task-oriented person. Deep down, I have always loved literature, but "sitting around reading" just didn't feel like I was being productive—especially since I have a child with a tracheostomy and feeding tube, a child recovering from his 18th surgery, others in high school working on college admissions, etc.

But the last seven years things started to change. I began to read again, I devoured *Pride and Prejudice*, *Kristin Lavransdatter* (gut wrenching, life-changing reading with that one) and Flannery O'Connor. I heard about Well-Read Mom when someone casually mentioned it on Facebook. I immediately looked it up and was beside myself that something like this existed. I signed up immediately, midway through the 2014-15 year, Year of the Spouse.

I moved to Atlanta from Michigan two-and-a-half years ago. After the dust settled, I asked around if anyone would be interested in starting a Well-Read Mom group and meeting at my house. My facilitating a group here isn't just about me reading great books. It's about building a community of women who read great literature, discuss big ideas, and go back to their families with their imaginations expanded, and feeling part of something much bigger than themselves. We are each changing culture, one book at a time, one discussion at a time. We go back to our teens and converse about something beyond schoolwork and schedules. We sit up at night and talk to our husbands about ideas beyond bills and kids. We watch our littles playing (or hear them bickering) and think of so many strong women we have read about, like Hannah Coulter, who show up and do the hard work of raising families and building strong communities, but often hidden away without fanfare or recognition.

Women's hearts are meant to go deep. We are meant to filter the world's (often unhealthy) call to our families' souls. But if we aren't able to think beyond laundry and grocery runs, the ground beneath us grows dusty and arid. We can stand firm against the battering that life brings us when our minds are filled with stories of fortitude, cautionary tales of free will run amok, lighthearted moments of joy as well as moments of intense grief.

I believe the reason great literature resonates so deeply with us is that we are all part of The Great Story. We are all in the epic battle between good and evil. We are all involved in salvation of our souls and those around us. Time spent tending to our souls isn't isolating but fortifying. It isn't selfish; it's self-preserving so we can tend to those in front of us.

Having my Well-Read Mom group has kept me anchored during

some pretty trying times. So often, as women, we easily fall prey to the "woe is me" themes in conversations. Our meetings aren't a time to be self-indulgent about our own issues, but to look beyond and reflect through a different prism of life, to be challenged to think beyond just "liking" or "not liking" a book to thoughtfully articulating how the book moved us.

On Writing Letters to My Children
by Ann Keiper

I love the WRM book group. In so many ways, it has made me a better mom, a better wife, a better friend, and a more faithful person.

After reading and discussing *Gilead* with the group, I have a new tradition with my children, who are now 15, 16, and 20. In the book, John Ames, who is in his 70s and dying, decides to write a long letter to his seven-year old son. The novel is the letter, in diary form, where he shares his memories, thoughts, experiences, philosophy, and faith— in hopes that later, his son will read and reflect upon it. After reading the book, I wanted to start writing actual letters to my children, with a goal of doing it every three-to-four months. I have been doing this for my three children since we read *Gilead* in our Well-Read Mom group. When a few months go by, my children sometimes observe, "Mom, you haven't written one of your letters to us lately."

I include three things each time I write them: 1) I recall a memory they may not remember or know about, 2) I tell them something about myself or about their dad and me as a couple, that they may not know, and 3) I give them a piece of advice on life, trying not to be nagging, but with the preface that even though I seem old to them, I have experiences and time on the planet, and I may actually have some good advice for them. The third piece often includes something about faith and how it plays a part in our lives.

I'm not sure if they will keep the letters, or re-read them someday when I'm gone, like John Ames intended for his young son, but it's been a great learning experience to sit down and write to them several times a year. Here's a quote from *Gilead*: John Ames writes, "I imagine your 'child self' finding me in heaven and jumping into my arms, and there is great joy in the thought."

On an Examination of Conscience
by Judy Myers

I had major foot surgery that landed me on the couch for a good solid three weeks. It just so happened that our Well-Read Mom book club was reading *The Divine Comedy* by Dante. I hadn't been sure that I really wanted to tackle this major work, even though deep down I always had a desire to read it. Now I had incentive and direction, so with nowhere to go, I picked up the book and began reading. Once I got started I could not put the book down. For me it was a mixture of spiritual contemplation and awe that with so few words framed in poetry the author conveyed his story.

As a cradle Catholic, sometimes I think that my examination of conscience before the Sacrament of Reconciliation is not thorough or good enough. Maybe I don't take the consequences of sin seriously enough. Dante gave me a better understanding of the horror of sin and greatly improved my examination of conscience. I am so glad I read *The Divine Comedy*.

On Living with Intense Purpose
by Heather Arszman-Lamb

I believe that Well-Read Mom has impacted my faith in a variety of ways, most profoundly through my reading of *The Secret Diary of Elisabeth LeSeur*. I've always tried to work on something within myself monthly, but then I discovered Elisabeth. What an incredible, inspirational woman—to live a life that is so rich and deeply humble and determined. Elisabeth lived her life with intense purpose, to work on her own virtue, and to help save those around her. What!?! I've heard of priests doing such crazy things, but for a layperson who is struggling with her own issues to offer up all of her struggles—struggles that profoundly affected her—to offer them up for ungrateful, unknowing irreligious people who mocked her, made fun of her, and berated her for her faith. What!?! I couldn't do it, wouldn't do it. That's what I thought.

Then I saw it. I felt it. This is indeed how you are to live your life. To be humble. To love with such intensity, with the deepest core of your being—with your soul. To give everything you have for those you love. To determinedly work on your own virtue despite the contempt of those around you. To give it your all. Every day.

I would never have discovered Elisabeth LeSeur without WRM, and I know I will never be her. But I can look to her as an awesome example of a determined, virtuous Catholic woman. Because of her, I will work to be a better person and to live my life with more purpose.

On Challenging Preconceptions
by Alison F. Solove

Mary has always seemed so distant, so other. Mary's life was nothing like mine; her holiness seems both completely alien and hopelessly out of reach.

And then Marcie announced that Caryll Houselander's *Reed of God* would be our December selection for The Year of the Contemplative. I would never, ever have picked up a book about Mary on my own.

For years I've sought a saint whose life looked anything like mine. *Reed of God* presents Mary as the most like us of all the saints. Many saints are called to something extraordinary; Houselander reminds her readers that Mary was called to live an ordinary life with extraordinary sanctity. As she explains, "[Mary] was simply to remain in the world, to go forward with her marriage to Joseph, to live the life of an artisan's wife, just what she had planned to do when she had no idea

145

that anything out of the ordinary would ever happen to her."

Mary's holiness is surely something I will never attain, but the example she sets is something familiar, a quest I can embark on, a way my life can be sanctifying.

To me, that's one of the greatest gifts of Well-Read Mom—having my preconceptions challenged by perspectives I might have ignored or rejected. Sometimes the challenge comes from books. Sometimes it comes from the women who are reading alongside me—who very often are models and guides to holiness themselves.

On Following an Attractive Proposal
by Marcia Otto

Two years ago, some of us from Houston attended a WRM presentation at the New York Encounter, where a beautiful Italian woman was giving a presentation on the book *The Betrothed*, by Alessandro Manzoni. I went there expecting a book presentation, but was surprised by this woman describing how much she understood about her life, her role as a wife and a mother, through reading that book with a group of friends. I immediately thought, *I want that for me. I want to understand more about myself and the reality surrounding me just like she did.* I subscribed to WRM, bought all the books, and came back to Houston with a plan. I started to read the first book, couldn't finish it, started to read the second book, couldn't finish it, continued my busy life, forgot about it.

Year of the Spouse ended, and one day I received at home the materials of the upcoming cycle: the Year of the Worker. I was struggling with a new job, but knew the proposal spoke directly to me. I also knew that I could not just buy the books and read them on my own; it would not last. A glimpse of a desire and a plan alone were not enough, I needed someone to accompany me. One day I approached my friend Serena and said, Do you remember that presentation? Do you think we can do something like that in Houston, a small group? Serena's face lit up: she too had had that desire for some time. She started to invite other friends. It became clear that the desire to read good literature is very common among women. There was no need to explain much.

WRM Houston is an answer to a long-time desire, partially known, and mostly discovered as I followed an attraction.

On the Reading-Motherhood Connection
by Erin Murphy

I joined my WRM book club when it started, halfway through the first year, Year of the Daughter. Around that time, my husband and I were beginning to explore the difference between leisure and entertainment, and considering how we could model the importance of leisure to our young children. The night of our first meeting, I came home very excited after listening to the first audio. Yes! The idea that I would be a better wife and mother by taking the time to read more struck me, while at the same time calmed me, because I could see that it was the truth.

Fast forward two years (and another extended period of sleep deprivation as we were blessed with another baby). My husband and I sat in our living room reading on a Sunday afternoon. Our six-year-old daughter, a fledgling and frustrated early reader, wordlessly sat down with us and opened her book and read too. Much joy abounded!

I've observed changes in myself, which I've really only appreciated these past few months. I read. A lot. And I enjoy it. I am no longer shy or afraid to share my thoughts about books (or movies or ideas). I believed throughout high school and college that I just "wasn't good at literature," but now I see that wasn't even the point. The point isn't to get an A on a test, or to add some wonderfully insightful comment to a discussion. It is simply to grow as a person, and to share this growth with my community, especially the sisterhood of mothers whom I'm privileged to encounter in this phase of my life.

On Living Marriage
by Rachel Digman

The Secret Diary of Elisabeth Leseur has been a touchstone in my marriage. When I feel discouraged and disconnected from my husband or feel that we are working at cross purposes, particularly when it comes to faith, I recall Elisabeth. How did she respond when her husband actively persecuted her for her religious beliefs? She persevered in her faith, and she met this persecution with two things: silence and prayer. She did not fight back, argue, or leave her marriage. She remained faithful to her beliefs and to her husband. And it was through her persistence in silence and prayers that her husband came to find Christ for himself. While her response may not be the correct one for extreme difficulties in marriage, for those of us weighed down by the day-in-and-day-out arguments, criticisms, and obstacles, it seems to be a wise path to consider. I pray that I can follow in her example. This book held a key for me for sustaining my marriage and allowing it to thrive.

On the Moral Imagination
by Rose Klassen

This is my seventh year with Well-Read Mom, and after that time of being challenged to read deeply and to converse with my friends about the characters and ideas, I can feel the moral imagination awakening in my soul. Now my imagination informs my relationships with family, friends, and community. I meet various characters and fall in love with them, or reflect upon their lives in such a way that they provide an opportunity of self-examination. If some event or some protagonist troubles me, I must ask, Why? In the asking—rather than a comfortable dismissal—I am urged to look into my heart and wonder, Is this a defect that is reflective of my life? If so, how can a change be made? These are questions essential to the formation of the imagination. We are drawn out of ourselves to love, since admiration for a hero or heroine inspires us to imitate his/her life's choices for the beautiful, good, and true. As the late Professor Kalpakgian said, think of the hero or heroine you love best. Do they not carry out all the corporal works of mercy? When we read and fall in love with a character, it is an incarnational moment; the word on the page takes on flesh. Christ meets us through the creativity of the novel in its characters, and He draws us out of the shadows, placing in our hearts and minds the desire to live better because we have encountered truth.

Love that comes to us in the form of friendship is also integral to the development of the moral imagination, as the *Divine Comedy* makes it clear. After their long journey together through the gaping hell-mouth and Purgatory, Virgil tells Dante that he will only accompany him to the end of Purgatory. Dante gazes at Virgil's face and begins to weep because he feels so deeply what a friend Virgil has been to him. I, too, was moved near to tears in company with Dante because I had come to love Virgil.

Dante's journey was not just through a fantastical Hell, Purgatory, and Heaven where he arrogantly judged the lives of others. Rather, he was on a pilgrimage through his own soul. By considering his love for others and the misdeeds of others, he was examining his own conscience. And he was appointed a friend and mentor to go with him. So, too, are we given friends as we travel on this path through the soul where together we grow to appreciate the mystery and beauty of the books, of each other, and even perhaps the opportunity to be a part of each other's salvation story.

On the Journey of Marriage
by Carla Galdo

How striking it is to see the effect that lived years can have on one's appreciation of a work of literature. I first read *The Jeweler's Shop* eight years ago, when I was still in the early years of my marriage. The story of Teresa and Andrew, engaged and hopeful, finding their whole existence "[standing] before Him," before Christ, is what resonated with me most.

Like Teresa and Andrew, I believe that my husband and I both stood before the "gentle and penetrating" eyes of Christ, and, responding to his call, entered into the vocation of marriage with sincere and hopeful trust. I saw the strong foundation upon which we stood, our shared faith, our love of Christ and his Church, and I thought building a life together would be, if not easy, at least straightforward.

Looking back, perhaps in truth I was, as Adam says in Act III, "blinded ... not so much by the force of [my] emotion as by lack of humility."

Four children, six houses, and one decade later, my husband and I found ourselves nearly strangers, both so often guilty of Stefan's distance and Anna's cool silence. We had "slip[ped] over such an edge . . ." and found it "very hard to get back," wandering "alone below the road [we] should be on," as the Chance Interlocutor comments in Act II.

Both desiring to find the way back, both not quite knowing how, we ultimately found ourselves on a Retrouvaille weekend, a Catholic marriage retreat that helps couples heal their struggling marriages. It was an experience that would be, in essence, a wash in the healing waters of humility. Fifty couples were there, one hundred people admitting their brokenness, admitting that they needed someone to help take them by the hand and lead them back from the murky lower roads of side-by-side solitude and hurt silences. The leaders in our weekend were others who had survived great trials in their marriages, who had already been able to reach out and to say to one another, as Stefan did to Anna, "What a pity that for so many years we have not felt ourselves to be a couple of children. Anna, Anna, how much we have lost because of that!"

Throughout the weekend, the leaders shared their stories and their sufferings with us, in great candor and deep humility. In each of them we could see that "something new that was growing" in them that "did not 'taste' of love"—something distinct from the emotional rush of new love—a love that was slower, more dearly won, and more clear-sighted. Like the moment Anna recognized Stefan's face in the Bridegroom, and the moment Stefan finally reached his hand to Anna's shoulder, that weekend was our turning point, the moment when we became, as Anna said, "less burdensome" to one another, and when, entering together into the suffering that our marriage had become, we felt what Adam referred to as the "gradual calm" that came "in the course of time."

On Embracing Family Life
by Kristee Flynn

My life has had its share of crosses, with the biggest cross being family life. However, I know God is using my vocation as a wife and mother to sanctify me. With each book I read, I ask the Holy Spirit to enlighten my mind and open my eyes to see how He wants to use the characters in the story to speak to me. I realize they too, like me, have crosses. Although they may be living completely different lives from mine, I can learn from them. I've discovered ways to embrace my cross and live fully alive in the reality that has been given to me. May all women read more and read well by joining Well-Read Mom!

On Finding Peace at the End of the Day
by Laura Flaherty

For the past decade, I have wanted to develop the habit of doing an examination of conscience each night before bed. I tried different methods, but it just seemed like one more thing to do at the end of a long day. Often I would find myself asleep before I could examine my day. I thought it was the "right" thing to do, but there was nothing personal in it. There was no encounter with Love.

Then, during Year of the Friend, I read *I Believe in Love* by Fr. Jean C. J. D'Elbee, who writes, "Jesus, repair what I have done badly, supply for what I have left undone." My lovely sister, leader of our Well-Read

Mom book club, made me a prayer card with these words. It sat by my bed, and each night, I would read the words. It didn't take long for the words to be inscribed on heart. Each night, as I prayed these words, I found so much in my day that was done poorly or left undone. It hurt my maternal heart to reflect and see my impatience, rudeness, or lack of presence to my beautiful little ones. But now, as this reflection is combined with the words, "Jesus, repair what I have done badly, supply for what I have left undone," it brings peace and freedom to my heart, not distress. I see each situation that stings, and I see Jesus coming with the holy oil of His Love and pouring it into the situation. Then I see my broken heart, and my Beloved then comes to me and pours His Love over my heart, and as this balm flows over me, I fall asleep, healed and at peace.

On Hosting
by Lisa Bushey

Each month my six- and eight-year-old daughters look forward to hosting our Well-Read Mom group. They help me bake a loaf of pumpkin bread or make a batch of cookies. They pick up the errant Magna Tiles in the living room and carry in pillows and ottomans from the other room. They arrange candles and set out water glasses and a pitcher of ice water and prep the coffee. We arrange and rearrange the treat and water and flowers on the table until we are satisfied. They get into their pajamas and then anxiously wait at the top of the stairs saying, "Can we stay up until the ladies come?" They watch as the ladies arrive, get a drink and a treat and mingle. When their Auntie arrives, they race downstairs for "just a quick hug!" They hear bits of the audio intro playing as they slip out to get some water or brush their teeth before bed. I assume that sometimes they are still awake and hear the joining of our voices as we end the evening with Night Prayer.

Madame Auclair from *Shadows on the Rock* left a lasting impression on me. She believed so strongly in the gift of what we pass on to our children and the joy and glory of making a home and a way of life: "a feeling about life that had come down to her through so many centuries ... [t]he sense of 'our way'—that was what she longed to leave with her daughter."

I am grateful to Well-Read Mom for reminding me that I am made for greatness and for supplying the tools to educate my mind and to enliven the fire and passion within me through these incredible sources of truth, beauty, and goodness. Not only am I encouraged intellectually, emotionally, and spiritually by these books but my children are breathing in this atmosphere of creating an opening in their lives to gather around good literature as a frequent occurrence, to share their lives in community with others, and to grow through the reading and discussing of these great works.

On Seeing My Father in a New Light
by Kristi Degen

It had been a long time since I had read fiction or had challenged myself to read something that required effort without immediate satisfaction. (Yes, I am a millennial.) But after reading *Hard Times*, I sat there sobbing and in a puddle alongside dear Louisa as she crumbled before her father, who had done his best and raised her with utilitarian values, thinking he was doing right by her. I crumbled under the weight of my college debt, my attempts at an engineering background, my coveted "pieces of paper" that were supposed to get me success and wealth. I cried over the love I have for my father who, I know, under all of the perhaps mis-guidance, loves me—and only wants what is best for me, even if he (we) may have been misguided into thinking we were made simply for this world and its productivity and fleeting "happiness." If not for Well-Read Mom, I would have never even considered reading anything from Charles Dickens, let alone persevering through his challenging narrative and allowing it to penetrate my deepest understanding of what I am made for.

Appendix B

Well-Read Mom Reading Lists: The First Eight Years

"And men go abroad to admire the heights of mountains, the mighty waves of the sea, the broad tides of rivers, the compass of the ocean, and the circuits of the stars, yet pass over the mystery of themselves without a thought."
—St. Augustine of Hippo, *Confessions*

"If every tiny flower wanted to be a rose, spring would lose its loveliness."
—St. Therese of Lisieux, *Story of a Soul*

"Through all the world there goes one long cry from the heart of the artist: Give me a chance to do my best."
—Isak Dinesen, *Babette's Feast*

Year of the Daughter (2012-13)

- "The Birthmark," by Nathaniel Hawthorne

- "Introduction" to *A Memoir of MaryAnn*, by Flannery O'Connor

- *My Antonia*, by Willa Cather

- *Babette's Feast*, by Isak Dinesen

- *The Confessions*, by St. Augustine

- *Kristin Lavransdatter*, by Sigrid Undset

- *Story of A Soul*, by Therese de Lisieux

- *The Hawk and the Dove Trilogy*, by Penelope Wilcock

"And roots, if they are to bear fruits, must be kept well in the soil of the land."
—Pearl S. Buck, *The Good Earth*

"We ought not to be weary of doing little things for the love of God, who regards not the greatness of the work but the love with which it is performed."
—Brother Lawrence,
The Practice of the Presence of God

"I am no bird; and no net ensnares me: I am a free human being with an independent will."
—Charlotte Brontë, *Jane Eyre*

"We have all known the long loneliness and we have learned that the only solution is love and that love comes with community."
—Dorothy Day, *The Long Loneliness*

"The most exhausting thing in life, I have discovered, is being insincere. That is why so much of social life is exhausting; one is wearing a mask. I have shed my mask."
—Anne Morrow Lindbergh, *Gift from the Sea*

Year of the Mother (2013-14)

- "A Good Man is Hard to Find" and "Revelation," by Flannery O'Connor

- *The Good Earth*, by Pearl S. Buck

- *A Lantern in Her Hand*, by Bess Streeter Aldrich

- *The Practice of the Presence of God*, by Brother Lawrence

- *The Odyssey*, by Homer

- *Jane Eyre*, by Charlotte Bronte

- *Exiles*, by Ron Hansen

- *The Long Loneliness*, by Dorothy Day

- *Gift from the Sea*, by Anne Morrow Lindbergh

"I declare after all there is no enjoyment like reading! How much sooner one tires of any thing than of a book! — When I have a house of my own, I shall be miserable if I have not an excellent library."
—Jane Austen, *Pride and Prejudice*

"A few moments of meditation and recollection each morning in the presence of God transforms and perfumes the whole day, like flowers cast about when night comes, whose fragrance at dawn anoints everything they have touched."
—Elisabeth LeSeur,
The Secret Diary of Elisabeth LeSeur

"Bullies, oppressors and all men who do violence to the rights of others are guilty not only of their own crimes, but also of the corruption they bring into the hearts of their victims."
—Alessandro Manzoni, *The Betrothed*

"I fled Him down the nights and down the days
I fled Him down the arches of the years
I fled Him down the labyrinthine ways
Of my own mind, and in the midst of tears
I hid from him, and under running laughter."
—Francis Thompson, "The Hound of Heaven"

Year of the Spouse (2014-15)

- *Hannah Coulter*, by Wendell Berry

- *Pride and Prejudice*, by Jane Austen

- "Lilacs" and "The Long Ago," by Mary Lavin

- *The Secret Diary of Elisabeth LeSeur*, by Elisabeth LeSeur

- *The Betrothed*, by Alessandro Manzoni

- "The Hound of Heaven at My Heels," by Robert Waldron

- *The Jeweler's Shop*, by Karol Wojtyla (St. Pope John Paul II)

- *Anna Karenina*, by Leo Tolstoy

"Only solitary men know the full joys of friendship. Others have their family; but to a solitary and an exile his friends are everything."
—Willa Cather, *Shadows on the Rock*

"The first degree of humility is prompt obedience."
—Saint Benedict of Nursia, *The Rule of Saint Benedict*

"When the quarrel had finally worn itself out they had found themselves at opposite ends of the earth, though lying side by side in the same bed."
—Ole Rølvaag, *Giants in the Earth: A Saga of the Prairie*

"Nothing is so painful to the human mind as a great and sudden change."
—Mary Wollstonecraft Shelley, *Frankenstein*

"Above all, don't lie to yourself. The man who lies to himself and listens to his own lie comes to a point that he cannot distinguish the truth within him, or around him, and so loses all respect for himself and for others. And having no respect he ceases to love."
—Fyodor Dostoevsky, *The Brothers Karamazov*

Year of the Worker (2015-16)

- *Shadows on the Rock*, by Willa Cather

- *Ida Elisabeth*, by Sigrid Undset

- *The Rule of St. Benedict*

- *Giants in the Earth*, by O. E. Rolvaag

- *Helena*, by Evelyn Waugh

- *Frankenstein*, by Mary Shelley

- *The Brothers Karamazov*, by Fyodor Dostoyevsky

"Don't you want to be alive before you die?"
—Anthony Doerr, *All the Light We Cannot See*

"The moment you realize you are worrying, make very quickly an act of confidence: 'No, Jesus, You are there: nothing — nothing — happens, not a hair falls from our heads, without Your permission. I have no right to worry.' Perhaps He is sleeping in the boat, but He is there. He is always there. He is all-powerful; nothing escapes His vigilance. He watches over each one of us 'as over the apple of His eye.' He is all love, all tenderness."
—Jean C. J. d'Elbée, *I Believe in Love: A Personal Retreat Based on the Teaching of St. Therese of Lisieux*

"It's the job that's never started as takes longest to finish."
—J.R.R. Tolkien, *The Lord of the Rings*

"Look at everything always as though you were seeing it either for the first or last time: Thus is your time on earth filled with glory."
—Betty Smith, *A Tree Grows in Brooklyn*

"Indeed the safest road to Hell is the gradual one — the gentle slope, soft underfoot, without sudden turnings, without milestones, without signposts, ... Your affectionate uncle, Screwtape."
—C.S. Lewis, *The Screwtape Letters*

Year of the Friend (2016-17)

- *The Death of Ivan Ilych*, by Leo Tolstoy

- *All the Light We Cannot See*, by Anthony Doerr

- *I Believe in Love: Retreat Conferences on the Interior Life*, by Jean D'Elbee

- *A Tree Grows in Brooklyn*, by Betty Smith

- *The Screwtape Letters*, by C.S. Lewis

- *Till We Have Faces*, by C.S. Lewis

- *The Lord of the Rings: The Fellowship of the Ring*, by J.R.R. Tolkien

"Not much time for prayer these busy days. Only the short ones. And not much time to think of self either; or comfort — physical, spiritual, or mental. So that is good, too. 'Self' is the great enemy. 'Deny yourself, take up your cross and follow me.'"

—Dorothy Day, *On Pilgrimage*

"Consider your origin. You were not formed to live like brutes but to follow virtue and knowledge."

—Dante Alighieri, *The Divine Comedy*

"This mountain is so formed that it is always wearisome when one begins the ascent, but becomes easier the higher one climbs."

—Dante Alighieri, "Purgatorio"

"Open your mind to what I shall disclose, and hold it fast within you; he who hears, but does not hold what he has heard, learns nothing."

—Dante Alighieri, "Paradiso"

"Grandpa had made the Lord seem so real, I wouldn't of been surprised if he'd said good night to Him. But after a long pause he just said a-men."

—Olive Ann Burns, *Cold Sassy Tree*

Year of the Pilgrim (2017-18)

- *Gilead*, by Marilynne Robinson

- *O Pioneers!* by Willa Cather

- "Revelation" and "A Good Man is Hard to Find," by Flannery O'Connor

- *On Pilgrimage*, by Dorothy Day

- *Strangers and Sojourners*, by Michael O'Brien

- *The Power and the Glory*, by Graham Greene

- *The Divine Comedy*, by Dante Alighieri

- *Cold Sassy Tree*, by Olive Burns

- *Les Miserables*, by Victor Hugo

"You don't understand. You've never hated anybody."
"No, I never have. We're allotted just so much time on earth, and I wouldn't want the Lord to see me wasting mine in any such manner."
—Truman Capote, "The Thanksgiving Visitor"

"There are only two kinds of people in the end: those who say to God, "Thy will be done," and those to whom God says, in the end, "Thy will be done." All that are in Hell, choose it. Without that self-choice there could be no Hell. No soul that seriously and constantly desires joy will ever miss it. Those who seek find. Those who knock it is opened."
— C. S. Lewis, *The Great Divorce*

"But the effect of her being on those around her was incalculably diffusive: for the growing good of the world is partly dependent on unhistoric acts; and that things are not so ill with you and me as they might have been, is half owing to the number who lived faithfully a hidden life, and rest in unvisited tombs."
—George Eliot, *Middlemarch*

Year of the Contemplative (2018-2019)

- "The Dream of Rood," author unknown

- *An American Childhood*, by Annie Dillard

- *My Name is Asher Lev*, by Chaim Potok

- A Christmas Memory" and "The Thanksgiving Visitor," by Truman Capote

- *Reed of God*, by Carol Houselander

- *Hard Times*, by Charles Dickens

- *Seven Storey Mountain*, by Thomas Merton

- *The Great Divorce*, by C. S. Lewis

- *Middlemarch*, by George Eliot

"You cannot imagine how time ... can be ... so still. It hangs. It weighs. And yet there is so little of it. It goes so slowly, and yet it is so scarce."
—Margaret Edson, *Wit: A Play*

"History often resembles myth, because they are both ultimately of the same stuff."
—J.R.R. Tolkien, *On Fairy-Stories*

"Love Jo all your days, if you choose, but don't let it spoil you, for it's wicked to throw away so many good gifts because you can't have the one you want."
—Louisa May Alcott, *Little Women*

"All shall be well, and all shall be well and all manner of thing shall be well."
—Julian of Norwich, *Revelations of Divine Love*

"The greatest honor we can give Almighty God is to live gladly because of the knowledge of his love."
—Julian of Norwich, *Revelations of Divine Love*

"Some people's blameless lives are to blame for a good deal."
—Dorothy L. Sayers, *Gaudy Night*

Year of the Artist (2019-20)

- *Wit: A Play*, by Margaret Edson

- T*he Picture of Dorian Gray*, by Oscar Wilde

- "Leaf by Niggle" and "On Fairy Stories," by Tolkien

- *Return of the Prodigal*, by Henri Nouwen

- *Little Women*, by Louisa May Alcott

- *Their Eyes Were Watching God*, by Zora Neale Hurston

- *Revelations of Divine Love*, by Julian of Norwich

- *Angle of Repose*, by Wallace Stegner

- *Song of the Lark*, by Willa Cather

- *Gaudy Nigh*t, by Dorothy Sayers

JOIN THE MOVEMENT OF WOMEN
CHANGING THE CULTURE
ONE BOOK AT A TIME!

Well-Read Mom (WRM) is a book club for women who want to accompany one another in reading the classics, great books, and timeless spiritual works from the Western and Catholic traditions. Our book selections for each year correspond to the themes of a woman's life: mother, daughter, sister, friend, worker, pilgrim, contemplative, and artist.

Learn More & Stay Connected

Find us on Facebook
or Visit
WWW.WELLREADMOM.COM

About the Author

Marcie Stokman is founder and president of the international movement and book club Well-Read Mom (WRM). With a passion for reading and motherhood, she writes and speaks to encourage women in a world of rising isolation, loneliness, and mental health issues. Through the power of reading together and reading well, Well-Read Moms across the country are finding friendships, meaning, and purpose in their WRM book clubs. Connecting on a deeper level and serving others in their search for purpose is Marcie's passion.

Marcie has a Bachelor of Nursing from the University of Nebraska, Kearney and Masters in Psychology from the Adler Institute in Chicago. As a clinical nurse specialist (CNS) in mental health, Marcie founded the Family Consulting Services at Cuyuna Regional Medical Center, which continues to operate today, providing individual, marriage and family counseling. She co-founded Frameworks, a workshop series for teachers, nurses, and the broader community on healthy lifestyle strategies and mindset habits.

Speaking and leadership credits include the Minnesota Association of Catholic Homeschooling Educators Conference (MACHE), the annual WRM conferences at the University of St. Thomas, St. Paul, Minnesota, as well as numerous organizations in Chicago, Milwaukee, Boston, New York, DesMoines, Denver, Sacramento and smaller cities across the United States and Canada.

Well-Read Mom hosts events for The New York Encounter, an annual Cultural Event. Discussions included C.S. Lewis' Screwtape Letters, Karol Wojtyla's The Jeweler's Shop, and Manzoni's The Betrothed. In 2018, Marcie facilitated a panel discussion on "An Epidemic of Loneliness."

Marcie's passion for the power of deep reading to transform lives and communities is central to her concerns and activism. Her training as a clinical nurse practitioner in mental health gives her a keen ear for listening and engaging in problem-solving and encouraging women in finding their passion and purpose. As an author, national speaker and panel facilitator, she seeks to awaken the best in women and families, re-vitalizing our culture through her mission to support more women to **Read More** and **Read Well**.

As a homeschool mom for twenty-five years, Marcie co-founded a classical co-op for high school students, bringing families together to support each other in their vision for excellence in education and seeking truth, beauty and goodness through the Western classical tradition. Marcie and her husband Peter have seven children and eleven grandchildren and reside in Crosby, Minnesota.